T0347495

The Internet and Parliamentary Democracy in Europe

This book investigates the ethical challenges the internet presents to contemporary parliamentary democracy in Europe and how these challenges are being addressed. It fills an important gap: current literature until now has largely focused on the study of internet usage by politicians and institutions. With the ever widening scope of participation in internet-based communication, there are widely differing views on its potential social, economic and political impact, and whether parliamentary democracy will be strengthened or weakened in the information age. Key questions include:

- To what extent is the internet being used in parliamentary political communication?
- Should there be any institutional control and monitoring of parliamentarians' use of the internet?
- What impact does the internet have upon the principle of trust and transparency in the context of parliamentary democracy?

The book compares four European parliaments in Europe: the British, European, Portuguese and Swedish Parliaments, using both quantitative methods (questionnaires and survey of websites) and qualitative methods (workshops and face-to-face interviews with parliamentarians and parliamentary staff).

Xiudian Dai is senior lecturer in politics of the new media in the Department of Politics and International Studies at the University of Hull. Dai has published widely on the politics of new media technologies, including The Digital Revolution and Governance (Ashgate, 2000) and Corporate Strategy, Public Policy and New Technologies (Pergamon, 1996).

Lord Norton of Louth [Philip Norton] is Professor of Government in the Department of Politics and International Studies at the University of Hull. Lord Norton is author or editor of 26 books. He is an internationally recognised expert on the British Parliament and on comparative legislatures.

Library of Legislative Studies
Edited by Lord Philip Norton of Louth, University of Hull, UK.

1. National Parliaments & the European Union
Edited by Philip Norton

2. The New Parliaments of Central & Eastern Europe
Edited by David M. Olson & Philip Norton

3. Members of Parliament in Western Europe
Edited by Wolfgang C. Muller & Thomas Saalfield

4. The New Roles of Parliamentary Committees
Edited by Lawrence D. Longley & Roger H. Davidson

5. Conscience and Parliamant
Edited by Philip Cowley

6. Parliaments & Governments in Western Europe
Edited by Philip Norton

7. Parliaments and Pressure Groups in Western Europe
Edited by Philip Norton

8. Parliaments in Asia
Edited by Philip Norton & Nizam Ahmed

9. The Uneasy Relationship between Parliamentary Members and Leaders
Lawrence D. Longley & Reuven Yair Hazan

10. Delegation and Accountability in European Integration
Edited by Torbjorn Bergman & Erik Damgaard

11. Second Chambers
Edited by Nicholas Baldwin & Donald Shell

12. Parliaments and Citizens in Western Europe
Edited by Philip Norton

The Internet and Parliamentary Democracy in Europe

A Comparative Study of the Ethics of Political Communication in the Digital Age

Edited by
Xiudian Dai and Philip Norton

Routledge
Taylor & Francis Group
LONDON AND NEW YORK

First published 2008 by Routledge
2 Park Square, Milton Park, Abingdon, Oxon, OX14 4RN

Simultaneously published in the USA and Canada
by Routledge
270 Madison Avenue, New York, NY 10016

Routledge is an imprint of the Taylor & Francis Group, an Informa business

© 2008 Edited by Xiudian Dai and Philip Norton

Typeset by Value Chain, India
Printed and bound in Great Britain by TJI Digital, Padstow, Cornwall

British Library Cataloguing in Publication Data
A catalogue record for this book is available from the British Library

ISBN 10: 0-415-45948-6
ISBN 13: 978-0-415-45948-8

Contents

List of Contributors

Xiudian Dai is Senior Lecturer in the politics and political economy of new media technologies, with particular reference to the European Union (EU) and China, at the University of Hull, where he is the coordinator of the e-Parliament research project (www.hull.ac.uk/e-parliament) and director of the postgraduate programme, 'The Internet and the New Economy'. He is currently conducting research on the use of new media technologies by the National People's Congress (NPC) and its members in China. Xiudian is the author of *The Digital Revolution and Governance* (Ashgate, 2000) and *Corporate Strategy, Public Policy and New Technologies* (Pergamon, 1996).

Cristina Leston-Bandeira is a Lecturer in Legislative Studies at the University of Hull. She has established herself as an expert on the Portuguese Parliament. She currently works on the relationship between parliament and the Internet, being the co-ordinator of a project that brings together academics and parliamentary officials from several European parliaments. Her recent publications include *From Legislation to Legitimation – The Role of the Portuguese Parliament*, 2004, and *Southern European Parliaments in Democracy* (editor), 2004.

Magnus Lindh is a Lecturer in Political Science at the Department of Political and Historical Studies, Karlstad University in Sweden. Alongside his research interests in the usage of information and communication technology (ICT) for political purposes, Magnus researches on how regional actors interact with the European Union. He co-ordinates the *Regions in a Globalised World* research programme at Karlstad and is a leading researcher in the Nordregio-funded *Fusing Regions? Sustainable Regional Governance and European Integration* research project. Recent publications include several articles in the Nordic international relations academic journal, *Cooperation and Conflict*.

Lee Miles is a Professor of Politics and Jean Monnet Chair in European Union Government and Politics at the School of Politics and Communication Studies at the University of Liverpool as well as being an Associate Fellow of Chatham House in London. He also holds a Docent in Political Science from Karlstad University in Sweden. In addition to writing on questions of European integration, Lee is regarded as one of UK's leading researchers on Scandinavian politics. Recent publications include, for example, *Fusing with Europe? Sweden in the European Union* (Ashgate, 2005), editor of the

Euro-outsiders special issue of the *Journal of European Integration* (2005) and three issues of the *European Union: Annual Review* (2003–2005).

Christine Neuhold is the Director of the Master of European Public Affairs and Associate Dean of International Affairs at the University of Maastricht. She has previously worked at the European Institute of Public Administration in Maastricht and the Institute for Advanced Studies in Vienna. Her research interests reach from the Institutional Framework of the European system to Comitology. Her publications include: (Routledge, 2006) 'Comitology as a Feature of EU Policy Implementation and its Effects on the Democratic Arena', in: Benz and Papadopolous (eds.): *Governance and Democracy – Comparing National, European and Transnational Experiences*; and (Edward Elgar, 2007), *Dynamics and Obstacles of European Governance* (joint editor with D. De Bievre).

Philip Norton [Lord Norton of Louth] is Professor of Government, Director of the Centre for Legislative Studies, and Head of the Department of Politics and International Studies at the University of Hull. His most recent publications include *Parliaments in Western Europe* (3 vols. 1998–2002), *Parliament in British Politics* (2005), and (with others) *Politics UK*, sixth edn. (2006). He was elevated to the peerage in 1998. He chaired the Constitution Committee of the House of Lords from 2001 to 2004 and is a member of the Select Committee on Regulators and the Law and Institutions Sub-Committee of the European Union Committee. He is President of the Politics Association and a Vice President of the Political Studies Association of the UK.

Jamal Shahin is a Lecturer, University of Amsterdam and Vesalius College (Brussels); Senior Visiting Consultant at the Danish Technology Institute and Senior Associate Fellow at the Institute for European Studies (VUB). Recent research has focused on the new governance debate in the EU, eGovernment in the EU, and the performance of the EU in international institutions. Recent publications include: 'The reassertion of the state: governance and the information revolution' in M. Dunn, S.F. Krishna-Hensel and V. Mauer (eds.) *The Resurgence of the State: Trends and Processes in Cyberspace Governance* (2007); 'A European History of the Internet' *Science and Public Policy* (November 2006); 'The EU's use of the Internet', in the *Encyclopedia of Digital Government* (2006).

Mª Rosa Vicente-Merino is a PhD candidate at the University of Hull, where she investigates the usage of the web by European political parties. She is also the research assistant of the project 'The Ethics of Conduct: The Impact of

New Media on Parliamentary Behaviour in Europe' at the University of Hull. She presented the paper 'Parliamentarians' Websites across Europe: Usage, Networking and Interactivity' at the Seventh Workshop of Parliamentary Scholars and Parliamentarians – Wroxton College (July 2006). Her research interests focus on the impact of the Internet on political participation and the usage of new media by political actors.

The Internet and Parliamentary Democracy in Europe

XIUDIAN DAI and PHILIP NORTON

The Internet, a global network of computer networks, is arguably the largest and most democratic system that human beings have ever created.[1] This is largely because of (a) the absence of any central control mechanism or authority in the Internet architecture and (b) the power of the Internet, to a great extent, deriving from the constituent machines and users worldwide – the more computers connected to the Internet and the more users using the network the more powerful it is. Despite the concern over the uneven access to the Internet, or the so-called digital divide, between those connected and those disconnected,[2] the ever widening scope of participation in Internet-based communication is already beginning to attract the attention of both the policy and academic communities due to the significant social, economic and political impact that this process has generated.[3]

With the introduction of each major innovation in the history of information and communications technologies (ICTs), such as the telegraph, telephone, radio and television, there were new hopes and hypes about a change in politics. The same is applicable to the arrival of the Internet. It seems that the prospect which the fast growth and widespread of Internet technologies could lead to the introduction of electronic democracy (e-Democracy)[4], at least the consideration of it, makes this new medium far more exciting than any other type of ICTs. Much research has been done in recent years dealing with Internet-engineered democratisation, particularly in authoritarian countries.[5] There is also a growing body of literature considering the Internet as a tool for electioneering, with a focus on political parties' use of this new medium.[6] In this volume, however, our research interest is directed towards the deepening and widening of the understanding about the relationship between the Internet and the most important institution in a liberal democracy, namely, the parliament (and its elected members), in a European context.

Although better government will not be an automatic result of the use of ICTs, new technologies are viewed as 'an integral tool of strategies to revitalise governance and renew democratic culture'.[7] In many parts of the world, in particular the western industrialised countries, the use of ICTs is already affecting the main areas of parliamentary functions such as general office operation (through office automation), campaigning (through electronic campaigning) and networking (by exploring the networking potential of Internet technologies).[8] Optimists argue that the interactive nature of Internet technologies has the potential to reinvigorate the democratic process and re-engage citizens in politics against the background of growing voter apathy, including the possibility of creating new political processes.[9] Some have gone even further contending that the Internet age heralds the beginning of a process for creating a 'virtual parliament', 'online parliament' and 'virtual parties'.[10] Differing from this optimism, findings of some recently published empirical research suggest a rather dismal picture. In their study of online and offline political participation in the UK, Di Gennaro and Dutton argued that online political participation was reinforcing or even exacerbating existing inequalities in offline political participation by increasing the involvement online among those who are already politically active, thus disadvantaging those from the less educated and lower socioeconomic groups.[11] This finding is similar to that of Gibson, Lusoli and Ward, who argued that Internet-based political participation is largely applicable to the well-educated and wealthy men, so far as the UK experience is concerned.[12]

In contrast to political parties' and their candidates' strong interest in pursuing the use of new media technologies during the period of election campaign,[13] elected political representatives in the western liberal democracies are often criticized for not being in tune with the digital age. Gordon Brown, UK Chancellor of the Exchequer, admitted that politicians had failed to use the mass-communication potential of the Internet and they are 'operating in the slow lane of the information superhighway'.[14] Generally speaking, parliament and government are criticised for 'not adapting traditional political structures and processes to reflect society's increasing reliance on digital media' and this 'has resulted in these institutions becoming out of touch with the public'.[15]

Although there is no consensus in terms of explaining the reasons why some politicians are not motivated to use ICTs, or use ICTs more effectively, in engaging citizens, it is suggested in the academic literature that, first, the Internet as a new medium for parliamentary communication so far attracts only a small minority of voters who are already active and privileged and thus leads to the danger of simply exacerbating existing participating and engagement gaps in the parliamentary system.[16] Secondly, that there are politicians and bureaucrats who find e-Democracy disruptive and they do not want to make use of untried methods[17] – an argument that is seemingly difficult to reject. Finally, for those politicians who are prepared to test the potential of new technologies the warning goes that '[s]imply adding new electronic channels of communication to pre-existing structures or putting information online will not automatically produce a democratic nirvana'.[18] It is important, though, to pursue the reasons why e-Democracy is disruptive in the view of some politicians and this, in part, constitutes the purpose of our research.

RESEARCH QUESTIONS

The overall aim of this volume is to investigate the impact of new information and communications technologies, in particular the Internet, upon parliamentary democracy in Europe. Through a comparative study of four parliaments, the British, European, Portuguese and Swedish Parliament, this volume attempts to address such key questions as whether the Internet as a new tool for political communication, would help strengthen or weaken representative democracy; to what extent parliaments and parliamentarians in Europe are prepared to explore the potential of e-Democracy and who decides on how the Internet should be used in the context of parliamentary communication. More specifically, our research addresses three important dimensions of the impact of the Internet upon parliamentary democracy, namely, the practices, principles and rules related to the use of the Internet in a parliamentary context.

First, practices of online parliamentary communication: It is generally accepted that websites have already become the main public face of parliaments and they offer the greatest potential for external effect in how citizens see the institution.[19] By the same token, personal webpages and personal websites are also the public face of parliamentarians, through which citizens get information about and interact with their representatives. Therefore, it is important that we measure parliamentary promotion and parliamentarians' use of the Internet in communicating with the general public. To start with, empirical studies presented in this volume aim to establish whether the Internet has already been accepted by parliaments and parliamentarians as a preferred way of communication.

Secondly, principles of online parliamentary communication: What are the main factors that have prompted an increasing number of parliaments and parliamentarians to use the Internet? Do they believe that the Internet is indispensable to sustaining democracy in the information age? Is Internet engineered politics more democratic? In his philosophical analysis of the Internet Gordon Graham offers a challenging suggestion.

> If the availability and efficiency of the means of communication and expression are important elements in the realization of democracy, and if in the Internet we have an unprecedented good means of communication and expression, we may infer that the Internet puts within our grasp an unprecedentedly good form of democracy.[20]

We analyse the rationales behind parliamentary use of the Internet with a view for establishing the reasons why parliamentarians were engaged, or disengaged, in online communication. By identifying with whom parliamentarians communicate *via* the Internet and for what purpose they communicate online we attempt to answer the question whether the use of the Internet is advantageous or disadvantageous to representative democracy. In other words, is it desirable and practical to develop a 'parliamentary e-Democracy'?

Thirdly, rules of online parliamentary communication: Many believe that, '[i]n the field of communication, social responsibility is based on ethical codes of behaviour that have their roots in values.'[21] Are there any formal institutional control and monitoring mechanisms of parliamentarians' use of the Internet, so that important issues raised by this new medium could be addressed through institutional mechanisms? We discuss the institutional responses to the opportunities and challenges brought by parliamentary and parliamentarians' use of the Internet.

DATA AND RESEARCH METHODS

Methodologically, our research is focused on four parliaments in Europe: the British, European, Portuguese and Swedish Parliaments, using both quantitative and qualitative methods. Ideally, it would have been much better if we could study each Member State parliament in the EU but that would simply not be manageable through our research project. Instead, we decided to choose a small sample of parliaments for detailed study. The choice of the Swedish case was due to the consideration that Sweden is one of the Nordic countries that have the highest level of Internet penetration among their population. At the other end of the scale in terms of Internet penetration, Portugal is among the group of EU countries, where there is a relatively low level of Internet penetration. The UK sits in the middle of the two extremes. The addition of the European Parliament to the list of case studies offers us the opportunity to examine the use of the Internet by parliamentarians representing constituencies from all Member States of the European Union. On the whole, the choice of our case studies was guided by the understanding that parliamentarians who represent constituencies where a large number of people have access to the Internet are generally more advanced in the use of this new media technology than their colleagues, representing constituencies with a lower medium level of socioeconomic development.[22] It is hoped that, by comparing the experiences, practices and views of the four parliaments and their parliamentarians, a European perspective on the development of and issues about 'parliamentary e-Democracy' can be established.

In the existing academic literature, comparative data on the impact of the Internet upon parliamentary democracy in Europe are scarce. Among a very small number of academic works, Thomas Zittel has undertaken a study on parliamentarians' use of the Internet, which compares the German Bundestag, Swedish Riksdag and US House of Representatives.[23] On a larger scale, the results of an EU-funded research project on the use of ICTs by members of parliaments in Austria, Denmark, Germany, the Netherlands, Norway, Portugal and Scotland (complemented by the additional cases of Switzerland and the USA) have recently been published as a special issue in the journal of *Information Polity*.[24] While the *Information Polity* articles represent a significant contribution to the area of study, there is a need for expanding the scope of research and updating the empirical data due to the rapidly changing situation of parliamentary and parliamentarians' response to the digital revolution.

In order to make a contribution towards building up a European picture of parliament and parliamentarians' use of the Internet and exploring the ethical questions raised in this process, contributions in this special issue draw up empirical data derived from, among others, questionnaire surveys, website analysis, face-to-face interviews and research workshops involving academics and practitioners. First of all, a questionnaire on 'The Impact of New Media on Parliamentary Democracy in Europe', containing 11 questions, was conducted during the period February to May 2005. The questionnaire was sent *via* conventional post to each Member of the British, European, Portuguese and Swedish Parliament. The questionnaire survey was conducted in three languages: an English version (used for the British, European and Swedish Parliaments), French version (used for the European Parliament) and

Portuguese version (used for the Portuguese Parliament). To complement the posted hard copy of the questionnaire, electronic versions of it in different languages were made available on our research project's website (www.hull.ac.uk/e-parliament), so that parliamentarians could download an electronic copy in a language of their choice and return the completed questionnaire to the research team either through post or e-mail.

The choice of a combination of conventional post and the project website as methods, rather than e-mail, for disseminating the questionnaire was due to the consideration that, first, e-mails with an attachment would take up parliamentarians' inbox space and might get deleted immediately and, secondly, an e-mail sent in bulk to all members of a parliament could well become the target of anti-spam software and get filtered out.

Given the fact that parliamentarians are frequently asked to participate in various survey studies and they all have a very busy diary, the overall level of response to our questionnaire survey was satisfactory. In total, 241 questionnaires (or 12.1 per cent) were completed and returned, out of a total of 1,985 questionnaires distributed. The breakdowns of the four case study parliaments' responses are shown in Table 1. Swedish MPs scored the highest with a return rate of 23.9 per cent, followed closely by Portuguese MPs with 20.4 per cent. In comparison, the response rate of parliamentarians at the British and European Parliaments were much lower at 6.8 per cent and 8.5 per cent, respectively. Although we do not attempt to make complicated statistical analysis on the basis of the questionnaire survey, answers contained in the returned questionnaires have been coded into SPSS. The statistical results do provide us with important indications of parliamentarians' use of the Internet and their views on the impact of this new medium upon parliamentary democracy in both a national and European context.

The second method of our research was web content analysis. During the process of research we analysed the official websites of the four case-study parliaments and the individual parliamentarians' own websites that are hyperlinked to the respective parliamentary website. The focus of our web analysis was on the interactive features of these websites, such as availability

TABLE 1
RESULTS OF QUESTIONNAIRE SURVEY

	Distributed questionnaires	Returned questionnaires	Of Total return (%)	Return rate (%)
British Parliament	659	45	18.7	6.8
European Parliament	732	62	25.7	8.5
Portuguese Parliament	230	47	19.5	20.4
Swedish Parliament	364	87	36.1	23.9
Total	1985	241	100.0	12.1

of e-mail contact, the use of hyperlinks and online communication facilities (for example, blogging, e-newsletters and online opinion polls). The results of the website analysis were used in assessing the extent to which parliamentarians were prepared and/or able to use the unique features of the Internet in parliamentary communication.

The third aspect of our methodology was interviews. To complement the quantitative data derived from the questionnaire survey and website analysis, the research team have undertaken a series of interviews with parliamentarians and parliamentary ICT staff at the four case-study parliaments. During the period June 2005 to August 2006, a total of 40 face-to-face semi-structured interviews were conducted in order to obtain qualitative data.[25] All interviews were guided by two lists of questions; one was addressed to parliamentarians and another to parliamentary ICT staff. With the consent of interviewees, all interviews were recorded and subsequently transcribed. With the exception of interviews at the Portuguese Parliament, which were conducted in Portuguese and then transcribed and translated into English, the rest were conducted in English.

Moreover, during the data gathering process three workshops were organised with parliamentarians, parliamentary staff and parliamentarians' assistants. These workshops have provided the opportunity for in-depth discussion between the research team and practitioners on issues related to the impact of the Internet on parliamentary communication.

Finally, in order to invite comments and feedback from both the academic community and practitioners on the initial findings of our research, earlier versions of most of the contributions included in this volume have been presented at international conferences such as the Seventh Workshop of Parliamentary Scholars and Parliamentarians at Wroxton College in 2006.

STRUCTURE OF THIS VOLUME

In order to examine the impact of new information and communications technologies, in particular the Internet, upon parliamentary democracy in Europe, the main research papers presented in this volume are of two types: detailed case studies on the relationship between the Internet and the British, European, Portuguese and Swedish Parliaments, on the one hand, and two horizontal and comparative studies, on the other. By pooling the survey data together, each of the two comparative papers is focused on one of the two most popular features of the Internet – the World Wide Web (WWW or web) and e-mail.

Our parliamentary case studies begin with the article by Philip Norton on 'Four Models of Political Representation: British MPs and the Use of ICT'. Building on a critique on Zittel's work on parliamentarians' use of the Internet,[26] Norton's article proposes and tests four models of political representation in the UK Parliament, namely, the traditional, political party, representative and tribune. Supported by first-hand empirical data, Norton explains the reasons why the party model of Internet use takes precedence over the other models in a British political context. In his contribution Norton provides a detailed and up-to-date account on the institutional and individual politicians' use of the Internet with a view to establishing the current pattern of e-Democracy development at the UK Parliament.

Compared with any national parliament, the European Parliament has a number of unique characteristics, including, among others, the location of the chamber across two geographical sites – Brussels and Strasbourg, supported by an administrative centre in Luxemburg. The article by Xiudian Dai on 'Prospects and Concerns of e-Democracy at the European Parliament' presents a detailed case study of the European Parliament's promotion of the use of ICTs in general and the Internet in particular to help reduce both the geographical distances and institutional boundaries in order to improve efficiency. Against this background, Dai's article seeks to answer the question of whether or not the search for e-Democracy through the use of the Internet has the endorsement by Members of the European Parliament. Bearing in mind the hopes and hypes about e-Democracy, research presented in Dai's article questions whether the Internet serves as a trustworthy medium for achieving the multiple goals, such as efficiency, transparency and accountability, of contemporary parliamentary democracy.

In order to deepen the understanding of the relationship between parliamentary democracy and communications technologies at the European level, Jamal Shahin and Christine Neuhold present a sub-case study on the impact of new ICTs upon the Standing Committees at the European Parliament. In their article, '"Connecting Europe": The Use of "New" Information and Communication Technologies within European Parliament Standing Committees', Shahin and Neuhold examine the process by which Internet technologies have become a focus of communication between a key part of the legislator, namely EP Standing Committees, and the outside world. A key question the authors try to address is, while helping key members of the EP Committees to fulfil their legislative role, does the Internet as a new communications tool provide any value-added to MEPs in functioning as representatives of European citizens? Drawing on evidences obtained from face-to-face interviews and the EP's official website, this article is intended to show how the key members of EP committees are responding to a growing volume of incoming e-mails.

Cristina Leston-Bandeira looks at the extent to which the use of ICTs could lead to changes in parliamentary activity in Portugal. More specifically, through examining the ways through which ICTs have been introduced in the Portuguese Parliament and analysing Portuguese MPs' perceptions of ICTs, Leston-Bandeira assesses the impact of ICTs on two general areas of parliamentary work: the parliament's relationship with citizens and the internal process of parliamentary work.

As a country where the levels of Internet penetration and ICT usage are among the highest in the world, Sweden constitutes an interesting case study in terms of the development of e-Democracy. In their article, which is provocatively titled 'Becoming Electronic Parliamentarians? ICT Usage in the Swedish Riksdag', Magnus Lindh and Lee Miles analyse Swedish MPs' usage of ICTs based on recently collected data against previous studies in the same field. This is followed by a discussion of the issues related to the role that political parties and parliamentary institutions play in promoting parliamentarians' use of ICTs. By emphasising the tensions between the individual parliamentarians, party organisations and parliamentary institutions in making use of the same ICT tools, Lindh and Miles explore the ethical challenges posed by the development of e-Democracy in a Swedish context.

Moving away from the single parliament case studies, the next two articles in this volume provide two different but complementary perspectives of the relationship between parliamentarians and the Internet, namely the web and e-mail.

The article by Rosa Vicente on 'Websites of Parliamentarians across Europe' offers a comparative analysis of parliamentarians' use of the Web at the British, European, Portuguese and Swedish Parliaments. The main concern of this article is to address such questions as how many parliamentarians have established a personal website and how interactive their websites are. Vicente starts with comparing the availability of parliamentarians' personal websites linked to their respective institutional websites of the four parliaments. This is followed by an attempt to compare the levels of interactivity of parliamentarians' personal websites with a view to establishing whether politicians in Europe are keen on exploring the potentials of two-way interaction online with voters or whether they are merely interested in one-way feeding of information about themselves to voters. Finally, Vicente discusses the reasons why parliamentarians are interested in creating their own website and some of the concerns raised by the use of interactive features of the Internet in the context of parliamentary communication.

Xiudian Dai's contribution, 'Political Ethics Online: Parliamentarians' Use of Email in Europe', provides another comparative study about the parliamentary politics of the Internet, with a focus on e-mail communication. The main questions Dai asks are how relevant parliamentarians consider e-mail communication to parliamentary communication; to what extent parliamentarians are actually using e-mail and what ethical issues have been raised by the use of e-mail in parliamentary communication. Dai starts by examining the extent to which politicians at the four parliaments covered in this volume perceive e-mail communication as a positive tool and are, therefore, prepared to make use of it. He then analyses the purposes for which parliamentarians use e-mail communication and their responses to received e-mails. Finally, he discusses some of the key ethical issues faced by parliamentarians in their use of e-mail communication.

This volume ends with a paper by the editors summarising the principal findings of the research and identifying directions for future research. It is hoped that this volume will mark the beginning of a joint endeavour between experts from the field of legislative studies and those specialising in the politics of new media to investigate the ways in which the digital revolution is unfolding in the context of parliamentary democracy.

ACKNOWLEDGEMENTS

The authors are grateful to the Institute of Applied Ethics (IAE) and the Faculty of Arts and Social Sciences at the University of Hull for the generous award of funding towards the research project 'Code of Conduct: The Impact of New Media on Parliamentary Democracy in Europe' (www.hull. ac.uk/e-parliament). Thanks also go to Kalsdad University in Sweden for their kind support towards the dissemination of questionnaires to parliamentarians in the Swedish Riksdag. We would like to thank the large number of parliamentarians, their assistants and parliamentary staff at the British, European, Portuguese and Swedish Parliament for contributing time and their personal views through responding to our questionnaires, answering our questions during interviews and participating in our research workshops. In particular, we would like to thank Dr Richard Corbett MEP and his office staff for having acted as our host during our field research at the European Parliament. Last but not least, the excellent research assistance provided by Rosa Vicente-Merino in the past three years is much appreciated.

NOTES

1. R. Davies, *The Web of Politics: The Internet's Impact on the American Political System* (Oxford: Oxford University Press, 1999).
2. The issue of digital divide between different countries and between different social groups remains one of the hottest debated topics related to the politics of the internet. See, for example, P. Norris, *Digital Divide: Civic Engagement, Information Poverty, and the Internet Worldwide* (Cambridge: Cambridge University Press, 2001); W. Wresch, *Disconnected: Haves and Have-nots in the Information Age* (New Brunswick: Rutgers University Press, 1996); L. J. Servon, *Bridging the Digital Divide: Technology, Community and Public Policy* (Oxford: Blackwell, 2002).

3. Among the many studies dealing with this topic, see M. Castells, *The Rise of the Network Society* (Oxford: Blackwell, 1996); M. Stefik, *The Internet Edge: Social, Technical, and Legal Challenges for a Networked World* (Cambridge, MA: MIT Press, 2000).

4. The term e-Democracy means the application of new ICTs, in particular internet technologies, and their transformational impact in political systems and processes. Other and comparable terms, such as digital democracy, cyberdemocracy and teledemocracy have also been used in the literature. For a detailed discussion of the origin and issues related to the concept of e-Democracy, see T. Vedel, 'The Idea of Electronic Democracy: Origins, Visions and Questions', *Parliamentary Affairs*, 59/2 (2006), pp. 226–35.

5. For instance, S. Kalathil and T. C. Boas, *Open Networks Closed Regimes: The Impact of the Internet on Authoritarian Rules* (Washington D.C.: Carnegie Endowment for International Peace, 2003). For the internet's impact upon democratisation in both established and new democracies, see P. Ferdinand (ed.), *The Internet, Democracy and Democratization* (London: Frank Cass, 2000).

6. See, for example, R. Gibson, P. Nixon and S. Ward (eds.), *Political Parties and the Internet: Net Gain?* (London: Routledge, 2003).

7. G. Lawson, *NetState: Creating Electronic Government* (London: Demos, 1998), p. 55.

8. R. Allan, 'Parliament, Elected Representatives and Technology 1997–2005–Good in Parts?', *Parliamentary Affairs*, 95/2 (2006), pp. 360–65.

9. See, for example, K. McCullangh, 'E-democracy: Potential for Political Revolution?', *International Journal of Law and Information Technology*, 11/2 (2003), pp. 149–61; R. Ferguson, 'How will the internet change politics?', Speech at Editorial Intelligence event, 29 March 2007, available at http://www.hansardsociety.org.uk/assets/Editorial_Intelligence_speech.pdf (accessed on 25 April 2007).

10. For reference to the term 'virtual parliament', see A. Campbell, A. Harrop and B. Thomson, 'Towards the Virtual Parliament – What Computers Can Do For MPs', *Parliamentary Affairs*, 52/3 (1999), pp. 388–403. Terms such as 'online parliament' and 'virtual parties' are discussed at length in Norris, *Digital Divide*.

11. C. Di Gennaro and W. Dutton, 'The Internet and the Public: Online and Offline Political Participation in the United Kingdom', *Parliamentary Affairs*, 59/2 (2006), pp. 299–311.

12. R. K. Gibson, W. Lusoli and S. Ward, 'Online Participation in the UK: Testing a "Contextualised" Model of Internet Effects', *British Journal of Politics and International Relations*, 7/4 (2005), pp. 561–83.

13. On the eve of the May 2007 UK local elections, virtually all political parties resorted to the internet to broaden their campaign coverage. Tony Blair launched the Labour Party's YouTube channel with a view to having direct communication with voters. Clippings of the Labour Party's election broadcast appeared on the same website ahead of the normal broadcast schedule. Likewise, other political parties in the UK have also been active in campaigning online.

14. Quoted in *The Times*, 27 January 2007.

15. 'Foreword' by Bridget Prentice MP in R. Ferguson, *Digital Dialogues* (London: Hansard Society, 2006), p. 7.

16. S. Ward, R. Gibson, and W. Lusoli, 'Old Politics, New Media: Parliament, the Public and the Internet', paper presented to the Political Studies Association Conference, University of Leeds, 5–7 April 2005.

17. S. Coleman and D. F. Norris, 'A New Agenda for e-Democracy', Forum Discussion Paper No.4, January (Oxford: Oxford Internet Institute, 2005), p. 24.

18. Ward, Gibson and Lusoli, 'Old Politics, New Media'.

19. Norris, *Digital Divide*, p. 133.

20. G. Graham, *The Internet: A Philosophical Inquiry* (London: Routledge, 1999), p. 66.

21. D. Newsom, *Bridging the Gap in Global Communication* (Oxford: Blackwell, 2007), p. 100.

22. T. Zittel, 'Political Representation in the Networked Society: The Americanisation of European Systems of Responsible Party Government', *The Journal of Legislative Studies*, 9/3 (2003), pp. 32–53.

23. Zittel, 'Political Representation in the Networked Society'.

24. For horizontal and comparative analyses see J. Hoff, Members of Parliaments' Use of ICT in a Comparative European Perspective', *Information Polity*, 9 (2004), pp. 5–16; P. Filzmaier, K. Stainer-Hämmerle and I. Snellen, 'Information Management of MPs: Experiences from Austria, Denmark and the Netherlands', *Information Polity* 9 (2004), pp. 17–28; G. Cardoso, C. Cunha and S. Nascimento, 'Ministers of Parliament and Information and Communication Technologies as a Means of Horizontal and Vertical Communication in Western Europe', *Information Polity*, 9 (2004), pp. 29–40; B, Elvebakk, 'Virtually Competent? Competence and Experience with Internet-based Technologies among European Parliamentarians', *Information Polity*, 9 (2004), pp. 41–53 and J. Hoff, 'The Democratic Potentials ff Information Technology: Attitudes of European MPs towards New Technology', *Information Polity*, 9 (2004), pp. 55–66. For single case analyses on the Scottish, German and Swiss Parliament see C. F. Smith and C. W. R. Webster, 'Members of the Scottish Parliament on the Net', *Information Polity*, 9 (2004), pp. 67–80; H. J. Kleinsteuber and M. Fries, 'German MPs and ICT', *Information Polity*, 9 (2004), pp. 81–7 and J-L. Chappelet, 'The Appropriation of E-mail and the Internet by Members of the Swiss Parliament', *Information Polity*, 9 (2004), pp. 89–102.
25. Note that the total number of interviews does not include the interviews conducted by Christine Neuhold and Jamal Shahin for their article.
26. Zittel, 'Political Representation in the Networked Society'.

Four Models of Political Representation: British MPs and the Use of ICT

PHILIP NORTON

There is no job description for a Member of Parliament in the UK. As with members of other legislatures, Members fulfil a range of tasks.[1] Most of those tasks, however, involve communication. At the heart of the traditional role is verbal communication in the chamber. Some wider communication, through correspondence and public speeches, is involved, though for much of the twentieth century the House of Commons had the characteristics of a 'closed' institution. Party served to cocoon Members and there was little need for them to engage in structured forms of communication with electors or bodies outside Parliament – certainly not on any extensive basis.[2]

Communication between MPs and electors became more extensive in the latter half of the twentieth century as demands on MPs increased. Constituents came to expect more of the local MP as a service provider. Greater volatility in electoral behaviour prompted MPs to pay more attention to their electoral base.[3] Resources were increased to enhance communication. In the mid 1960s, an MP had a salary and a locker; if he (rarely she) was lucky, he may have a desk. Even if an MP wanted to communicate with constituents, there were few resources available to do so. As one newly elected MP reported, his office was the front-room table in his home. This gradually changed. A secretarial allowance was introduced, which later developed into an office cost allowance, enabling an MP to hire staff and fund office equipment. The parliamentary estate was expanded, enabling each MP to have an office. The advent and growth of the Internet generated demands for PCs and Internet access. Computer facilities were introduced, albeit in a haphazard manner. MPs opted for different computers, creating problems with networking and compatibility.

Over recent years, ICT facilities have become both more extensive and more co-ordinated.[4] On 1 January 2006, a unified Parliamentary ICT service (PICT) was introduced, covering both the Houses of Parliament. Legislation was introduced in 2007 to provide authority for a joint department to manage ICT provision. PCs and other equipment are routinely supplied to MPs and their staff. Of the MPs elected in 2005, all but 29 had (by mid 2006) submitted orders for equipment.[5] Staff usage has increased significantly. The Palace of Westminster constitutes not so much a political village as a small town. Nearly 10,000 people work in it. MPs' (and peers') staff and parliamentary officials are now networked. In January 2002, there were 4,838 e-mail accounts on the Parliament.uk domain. By May 2006, the number was 7,397. These facilitate internal and external communication. For MPs, contact with constituents is especially important. Of computers supplied to Members, it is estimated that five per cent are located in Members' homes, 45 per cent in Westminster and 50 per cent in the constituencies.

Parliamentarians and their staff thus have access to the Internet. For most, it has become an essential aid to their daily activity. The same applies to many outside the Parliament. By 2005, 61 per cent of Britons were using the Internet.[6] The Internet offers the potential to link parliamentarians with electors in a direct and relatively inexpensive manner. It is innovative in terms of technology, and it has the potential also to be employed in innovative ways, reshaping the form of politics through facilitating new organisational forms and enabling citizens to express views directly to legislators, without the use of intermediaries such as journalists, editors and political parties. But to what extent has it transformed the lives of MPs, not just in terms of efficiency but also in terms of their roles as elected representatives? Has it served to re-define their relationship to those who elect them?

In his study of the use of the Internet by parliamentarians, Thomas Zittel proposes two models of political representation in a networked society: the technological and the constitutional.[7] The former sees the transformative opportunities of the Internet, helping create an electronic democracy and redefining the relationship between legislators and electors. Over time, new generations of parliamentarians are able to exploit the Internet to bypass party and to create a more direct, individual mode of communication.

The Internet is seen as being at the heart of communication and a challenge to existing forms of responsible party government. The latter model posits the use of the Internet as one of a number of means of enhancing existing political systems. In a parliamentary system, it will be utilised to bolster rather than challenge the position of parties as essential elements in delivering cohesion and a coherent programme of public policy. Here, the Internet is not used to redefine but to support existing relationships.

Zittel's findings suggest that the use of the Internet is shaped by the institutional design of a political system, giving some support to the constitutional model, but of the three countries he studied (the USA, Germany and Sweden), there was evidence in two of a generational effect, giving some support to the technological model. However, not all his findings met the predictions of either model and some of the findings remained unexplained. As he noted of the constitutional model, it may be under-simplified.[8] The purpose of this paper is to advance and test four models of political representation, influenced by, but going beyond, Zittel's dichotomised models. They are designed to see if we can get a greater purchase on ICT usage by MPs. The four models are the traditional, party, representative and tribune models.

The *traditional model* posits a rejection of the use of ICT as a means of reinforcing or changing existing modes of representation. Though the use of the Internet has expanded dramatically since the early 1990s and been utilised by parties and politicians as an important tool of communication, not all politicians have rushed to embrace it. This rejection may be borne of fear or comprehension. The former derives from a lack of knowledge of the Internet and its uses (not knowing). The latter derives from an understanding of what it entails (not wanting). MPs may have little or no knowledge of the Internet facilities. Even those who employ e-mail or the web may not be fully aware of its potential. (One researcher in 2000–01 reported that his MP asked: 'Can you check if today's e-mails have come in yet?') Those who know what it entails recognise its potential for adding to their workload rather than serving as a tool for enhancing efficiency. In this model, citizens are seen as necessarily excluded, since they have no means of contact.

The *party model* posits the dominance of party and that ICT will be employed in order to bolster the position of party in the political system. Where parties already are dominant in the system – most likely parliamentary as opposed to presidential systems – ICT will thus be used to reinforce existing means of communication. Though the technology itself may be innovative, the use to which it is put is not. The Internet is employed to ensure that the party message is conveyed electronically in addition to, or in place of, paper form. Communication at the individual level, between parliamentarians and citizens, will mirror that of traditional forms of communication, reinforcing the party position or at least not challenging it. In this model, the role of citizens is essentially passive, being the recipients of material made available via the Internet. Communication is primarily, though not exclusively, mono-directional.

The *representative model* derives from the distinction drawn between the MP as a representative and as a delegate. In the Burkean conception of representation, MPs owe electors the benefit of their judgement, acting on what they see as the interests of the nation rather than acting as a cipher for the views of constituents. When Burke generated his trustee theory, it was in order to justify Members acting independently of the views of constituents. Today, Burke's words are voiced at times when MPs wish to go against the party, be it local or national.[9] David Judge cites George Gardiner, the Conservative MP for Reigate who in 1996, facing calls for his de-selection after attacking the party leadership, declared: 'Reigate Conservatives will have to decide whether a Member of Parliament is sent to Westminster purely as lobby fodder, or whether he should exercise his own judgements on matters of supreme national importance'.[10] In this model, the Internet is used as a tool for disseminating the Member's particular views and for mobilising support for those views, enabling the MP to act as an independent entity or at least be less dependent on party than would otherwise be the case. Here, the Internet is employed not to reinforce existing means of communication but rather to create new channels that will enable the MP to bypass the party. This is more in line with Zittel's technology model and with the perceived experience of the Internet in some countries as a campaigning tool. In it, the role of citizens is seen essentially as reactive – having some engagement with the MP.

The *tribune model* sees the MP as acting as the voice of the people. The MP acts here essentially on the direction – or at least is motivated by the views – of others. The model, though, is distinguishable from the party model, for what is posited here is not acting on the prompting of the party but on the prompting of those who elected the MP. This is the model that most clearly parallels Zittel's technology model, for it posits the use of ICT to glean the views of constituents in a way that existing modes of communication do not permit. Local opinion polls are expensive and (for that reason, among others) rare. Letters from constituents are generally unsolicited and, certainly in the UK case, most often concerned with individual problems than the expressions of opinion on public policy. The Internet offers the opportunity for structured and direct interaction of MP and electors not possible since the days of a small population and a very restricted franchise – that is, before the advent of mass democracy.

The tribune model may not necessarily appear to ascribe much independence to the MP, but it is the one that is assumed to be most likely to enhance popular support for the political system through enabling citizens to have an input into the political process, bypassing the moderating effect of catch-all parties. Even if MPs do not necessarily follow the views expressed by constituents – or even if they do go with the majority view, those in the minority do not affect the outcome – constituents nonetheless have had an opportunity to feed in their opinions and be heard by their elected representatives. Indeed, the new technology can help foster a conversation between electors and the elected.[11] In such an interactive environment, MPs have the facility to respond and explain their actions and comment on the views that have been expressed. In this model, the role of citizens is seen as being active and indeed proactive.

From a rational choice perspective, the party model is the most plausible in the context of the UK. MPs are returned for individual constituencies, but the primary determinant of their election is party. It is, therefore, in their self-interest to maintain the position of their party. It is also in their self-interest to be constituency active. Though the potential for the incumbent to attract votes because of their personal appeal and activity – a 'personal vote' – is limited, it is not non-existent.[12] It can make a difference at the margins, and the margins can matter. Constituency activity may not change votes but it may help retain the votes of supporters who are otherwise inclined to switch their votes because of the unpopularity of the incumbent's party. The interests of the party and the MP coincide in terms of being active and being seen in the constituency. In the early years of the Blair Government, this coincidence was acknowledged with the party introducing a scheme for Labour MPs to be absent, on a rota basis, from Westminster and to spend a week in their constituencies in order to bolster their, and hence the party's, support.

The representative role also appears rational in that, those MPs who take an independent line are more likely to want to bolster their position and bypass their party. They are, therefore, likely to seek the support of constituents – MPs secure in their home base need not worry unduly about the party nationally – and of groups and individuals outside the constituency who can provide intellectual, political and material support.

The least plausible from a rational choice perspective are the traditional and tribune roles. From such a perspective, the traditional approach has little to commend it. It is not in the MP's self-interest to be cut off from an important form of communication, one that can speed up contact between the party and the MP and enable the MP to communicate information to constituents in a cost-efficient manner. There is little political capital for the MP or the party in being seen to reject a form of communication that is increasingly being employed by citizens and, indeed, for many becoming the principal form of communication with others, displacing the telephone and letters.

The tribune role also appears to work against the self-interest of MPs. However attractive it may be from a democratic perspective, enabling MPs to engage with citizens and to enhance popular support for the political process, it is not in MPs' interests, either politically or practically. Politically, it threatens the position of the party. If local opinion runs counter to the party's position, the party then has problems in ensuring that its Members stay in line. It threatens policy cohesion as well as party cohesion. Party cohesion enables government to deliver a coherent programme of public policy. MPs adopting the role of delegates on behalf of their constituencies have the potential to threaten that cohesion. (The situation is similar to that of referendums and is equally, in a strict sense, irresponsible.) However, the practical limitations are the most problematic. MPs already devote considerable time to constituency service. The demands of constituents have grown decade by decade. Though Members ascribe considerable importance to their constituency work – always giving it priority – it is demanding and may impinge on their collective role at West-minster. The greater use of ICT, especially for interactive communication, adds a considerable burden on top of the existing heavy workload. The benefit to the MP may be limited relative to the time and potential political costs.

TESTING THE MODELS

There are data available that enable us to test each model. The principal data, as employed by Zittel in his article and by other contributors to this volume, comprise the websites of MPs. Some data on the Internet use of the UK Parliament have already been researched and analysed by the Hansard Society,[13] as well as by Coleman,[14] Ward and Lusoli[15] and Jackson.[16] Analysis has also been undertaken by Vicente, as reported elsewhere in this volume. We draw on this work, but the principal source of our study is our own research of MPs' e-mail accounts and websites, encompassing quantitative and qualitative analysis.

Traditional Model

This model can be tested through the number of MPs with e-mail and websites. As may be inferred from the data already cited, there is little support for the model in terms of the number of parliamentarians who have resisted the onward march of the Internet.

Most MPs have e-mail accounts and websites. As we have recorded, only 29 MPs in the Parliament returned in 2005 did not order PCs and other equipment. Most MPs with PCs have access to the Internet and the overwhelming majority have e-mail accounts. At the end of 2006, only 21 MPs (three per cent of the total) did not have an e-mail link on the Parliament website or have an e-mail address listed in Dod's Parliamentary Companion.[17] Of the 21, five were Sinn Fein MPs from Northern Ireland who (because they refuse to take the oath of loyalty) had not taken their seats. The remainder comprised eight Conservative, five Labour and one Social Democratic and Labour Party (SDLP) MP. The Labour MPs included two Cabinet ministers and ex-Cabinet minister David Blunkett, who is blind.

Most MPs also have their own websites, with the number increasing parliament by parliament. As Vicente shows elsewhere in this volume, in 2004, 65 per cent of MPs were listed on the Parliament website as having their own individual websites; by early 2006 the percentage had reached 67 per cent. By the beginning of 2007, the figure was 73 per cent. (The increase may have been the consequence of a re-design of the Parliament website, introduced in September 2006, with more MPs linking their websites to it.) Of the 172 Members (27 per cent) in 2007 without a website, 100 were Labour (28 per cent of the parliamentary party) and 48 were Conservative (24 per cent of the parliamentary party). The biggest disparities occurred among the other parties. Among Liberal Democrat MPs, only ten per cent were without websites. Among parties from Northern Ireland, employing websites was a minority activity: of the 18 MPs returned from the province, only six had websites. Newly elected MPs tended to mirror the House as a whole, with 76 per cent having websites.

Most MPs thus embrace the use of new technology, especially for the purpose of correspondence. The traditional approach appears to have little support. However, the embrace is not necessarily enthusiastic: some MPs like to keep the Internet at arm's length. Not all appear keen to disseminate their e-mail addresses too widely. Although only 21 do have an e-mail link on the Parliament website or have an e-mail address listed in Dod's, it does not mean that the rest are linked via the website *and* in Dod's. On the Parliament website – the site more easily accessible to the public than Dod's – there were 81 MPs who had no e-mail link. Analysis of the e-mail addresses listed in Dod's shows that a number prefer to channel electronic correspondence through their office staff. Of MPs listing e-mail addresses in Dod's, 41 listed staff e-mail addresses. (56 also listed e-mail addresses other than parliament.uk addresses.) Of Members' websites, not all were active: 20 were inaccessible, or rather 18 were not accessible, one linked to an online poker site and another linked to a site listing Chihuahuas for sale. (Of the 20 sites, 17 were those of Labour MPs.) Another had not been updated in the previous 17 months.

There is, then, some wariness on the part of some MPs, in some cases borne of recognition of the potential increase in workload that it may entail. In 2002, the Information Committee of the House of Commons noted that, typically, '10 to 20 per cent of a Member's correspondence might be received electronically', adding 'but this figure seems set to climb'.[18] The use of staff to deal with e-mail correspondence, either through their own e-mail accounts or through the Members', is essentially a rational way of dealing with an increase in the volume of correspondence, which already places pressure on Members.[19] Some wariness is also borne of concern as to whether or not e-mail correspondents are actually constituents of the MP. By convention, an MP does not deal with particular problems raised by constituents of other MPs. It is not unusual to request e-mail correspondents to supply postal addresses. (Some Members reply to e-mails by letter, so as not to privilege e-mail over ordinary mail.) Workload implications may also explain why few MPs have blogs, an issue to which we shall return.

Some Members may be wary of the new technology, but they accept nonetheless that they have to utilise it. They employ their websites to advertise their availability; of the websites existing in 2004, 97 per cent listed the means by which the MP could be contacted. Of the 21 MPs not listing an e-mail address, not all are out-and-out traditionalists. Four of the 21 have websites. Of these, two do provide e-mail addresses. Also, of the four, two offer quick-poll facilities, one won the March 2005 Website of the Month Award, and one has now started his own blog. The embrace of the Internet by MPs may not always be enthusiastic, but it is moving in the direction of being pervasive.

Party Model

The party model can be tested primarily through looking at the use to which MPs put their websites. We would expect their use to reinforce existing modes of communication – geared to promoting the party and the work of the MP as the local Member – through disseminating the equivalent of constituency newsletters and press releases, in essence, the sort of material that the MP would like to see put through letter boxes or carried (but often is not) in local newspapers. Given that this is essentially promotional activity, we would expect the communication to be primarily one-way, with little or no interactive facility.

The websites are used essentially for three purposes: one is to promote the individual Member (through a biography, photo gallery, listing their speeches and views), a second is to promote the Member's views of constituency issues and the third is to promote the party. It is common to utilise a site to promote all three. Most active websites contain some party political content. Of the 443 active websites of MPs from the three main parties in 2007, 248 contained party political content on the home page: this extended beyond a party logo to include links to the national or local party, party material or even invitations to join the party. Invitations to join the party were standard on Labour MPs' websites created by the Labour Party. There was a clear party bias, in that the websites of Liberal Democrat MPs overwhelmingly had party links: of Liberal Democrat websites, 89 per cent had political content. Among Labour and Conservative MPs with websites, there was a fairly even divide: of Labour websites, more had political content than not (52 per cent to 48 per cent), whereas with Conservative sites 49 per cent had political content and 51 per cent did not. The ones with the least party content, and indeed with the least substantive content, were those hosted for MPs by ePolitix, part of Dod's Parliamentary Communications (51 MPs had ePolitix sites.) In some cases, these had little more than a biography of the Member.

Though most websites had some party political content, the principal content of the vast majority was constituency related, explaining what the MP was doing in the constituency and the issues that were being pursued. Most of the sites were standard static sites. Only one (that of Greg Pope, Labour MP for Hyndburn) had animation and audio when the home page was accessed. Most were essentially MP-centred and were designed to promote the Member.

The flow was essentially one-way. There was relatively little scope for interaction. Some had quick-polls on local issues, but they were notable for their rarity. As Vicente details in her study, over 80 per cent of the websites had low, very low or no interactivity. Only 28 per cent provided the opportunity for constituents to receive electronic bulletins: most of these were party bulletins or a mix of the party's and the MPs' bulletins.[20] It was not unusual for a site to give the Member's Westminster and/or constituency address, telephone number and e-mail address. Beyond websites, few MPs had their own blogs. The first MP to start a blog was Labour MP, Tom Watson, in 2003 (www.tomwatson.co.uk). The number has grown since, but remains extremely modest. At the beginning of 2007, Francoli and Ward identified 39 MPs who had blogs, 6.2 per cent of the membership of the House. (Just over half-a-dozen MPs also utilised social networking sites, such as Facebook and MySpace.)[21] Their study of the blogs revealed a particular diary theme. 'As part of this tendency, reporting of parliamentary activities such as contributions to debates, listing of questions they have asked, or accounts of parliamentary debates, featured quite highly.'[22] Interviews with MPs revealed that most Members would not consider criticising party or colleagues 'and suggested that MPs effectively self censor themselves'.[23]

Overall, then, the data are largely supportive of the party model. MPs use the Internet but essentially as a means of supplementing or reinforcing existing means of promoting themselves, and their parties, to constituents. Websites provide the means of making available material that MPs would like to send regularly to their constituents but are not able to do because of the financial or the labour costs: paper mailing is expensive and a marked decline in party membership in recent years has meant that it is more difficult than before to recruit volunteers to deliver leaflets house to house. The Internet has helped substitute for a declining capacity to reach constituents by other means. The salience of the party model is reinforced when we utilise data to test the remaining models.

Representative Model

The representative model can also be tested through the use to which Members put their websites. We would expect MPs who express views that set them apart from their party to utilise the Internet to develop and justify their views and encourage constituents, and others, to support them. For those especially keen to keep constituents and others regularly informed of their views and activities, and to engender a reaction, we would hypothesise that they would be the Members most likely to create blogs. As the Chief Executive of the National Council for Voluntary Organisations observed, blogs are a way of showing that organisations 'are connected with their grass roots'.[24]

In order to translate independence into empirically measurable form, we utilise data on voting dissension – that is, MPs who vote against their party. Recent years have seen a notable increase in dissent by back-bench MPs.[25] For the purpose of this analysis, we have taken the 114 Labour MPs to have cast one or more dissenting votes in the 2005–06 session of Parliament.[26] Our findings reinforce those of Ward and Lusoli, who found that the top rebels between 2001 and 2003 were less likely to have websites than the average MP.[27] MPs who rebel from the party line are less likely to have websites than party loyalists, and the more rebellious the MPs, the less likely they are to have a website.

Given Ward and Lusoli's findings, we tested the relationship between being a rebellious MP and *not* having a website. Utilising a Yule's Q index of association, we found a moderately positive association of þ0.35. (The values in Yule's Q range from 21.00 to þ1.00.) As we have seen, 73 per cent of MPs have websites. Among the 114 rebellious MPs, the figure is 63 per cent. The disparity, however, is most marked when we concentrate on the most rebellious MPs – those who voted against the Government twenty times or more in the session. Among these, only 50 per cent (8 out of 16) have websites.

One possible explanation for dissenting MPs not having websites is that they tend to be longer-serving MPs. However, as we have seen, the difference between newly elected Members and longer-serving Members in having websites is small. The relationship between being rebellious and not having a website also holds when one controls for the length of service. The 114 rebellious MPs include eight first returned at the General Election of 2005. Of these, three do not have websites, including one who falls into the category of the most rebellious Members and another who falls just outside (with 18 votes cast against the Government). All three are more rebellious than the rebellious new Members who have websites.

Given these data, it is perhaps not surprising that blogging has not been utilised much by rebellious Labour MPs or, indeed, as indicated in our earlier data, by Labour MPs generally. As Francoli and Ward note in their study, 'the data suggests that bloggers do not necessarily equate with rebels'.[28] Our study found two exceptions among the most rebellious MPs. Of these, though, one updates his blog intermittently (three entries for the first three months of 2007) and, at the beginning of April 2007, the 'campaigns' section of his website was empty and waiting to be updated.

However, the representative model cannot de discarded altogether. A few MPs do use their websites to explain their views on issues where they disagree with their party. Of the 25 most rebellious MPs with websites, eight use their homepages to signal their views. (The dissenting views of some others can be found by looking at their archived articles or speeches). However, only three of the 25 have an interactive capacity, that is, where people can comment online (as opposed to e-mailing comments); and one has a 'shout box'.

Thus, the MPs who use their websites to proclaim their views independent of party *and* seek to engage with those who visit their websites are exceptional. There is little evidence of MPs exploiting new technology to enhance their status independent of their parties.

Delegate Model

We can test the delegate model through the extent to which MPs use the Internet to elicit the views of constituents. We would expect MPs' websites to have a high degree of interactivity, enabling constituents to express their views online, either individually or through a dedicated vote-counter on a specific issue (as through a 'shout box'). As is apparent from the data we have already reported, there is little to support this model. We have already reported that 80 per cent of the Members' websites have low, very low or no interactivity. It is common for a website to list the MP's mailing address and (but not always) an e-mail address. Some have a capacity to e-mail the MP, with comments, from the website. However, as already noted, it is rare for a website to enable an on-screen interaction between MP and constituents. There are exceptions. David Drew, Labour MP for Stroud, for example, has a 'Have Your Say' section on his site, where visitors can post comments and he can respond, though at the beginning of April 2007, he had not responded to any of the comments posted since early February.

There is little or no evidence of MPs using the new technology to garner the views of their constituents and to do so systematically and in such a way as to influence their behaviour. Issues may arise through e-mail or online communication, but these tend to be the sort of constituency issues that would otherwise have been pursued through ordinary correspondence. Although MPs will variously articulate what they deem to be the views or interests of their constituents, they have no means of finding out what the majority view is in the constituency on a particular issue. The Internet provides a means, but an imperfect one, of seeking the views of constituents on public policy. There is little evidence of them using it for that purpose. Where they do, it has to be said that there is little evidence of constituents flocking to make their views known. There appears to be little obvious appetite to access MPs' websites. Data are limited, as few sites include counters for the number of visitors. Some do and a few record reasonably healthy numbers. David Drew's (interactive) website, for example, attracted just under 13,000 visitors between July 2004 and April 2007. Others record a handful.

Perhaps the best indicator of public interest is the number of comments on MPs' blogs. Our study confirms the findings of Francoli and Ward that few blogs attract a significant number of comments from visitors. In their study, nearly 40 per cent of the blogs received an average of less than two comments per posting. Only the more prominent MPs attract a significant number of comments. This was apparent from our study of blogs for the first three months of 2007 – only two, those of a senior minister (David Miliband)[29] and a high-profile Conservative front-bencher (Boris Johnson)[30], attracted a significant number of comments from visitors. Miliband had a total of 256 comments and Johnson had 509. Although a member of the Conservative front bench, Johnson had a reputation for speaking his mind (and consequently regularly covered in the tabloid press) and his Internet activity would put him in the representative rather than the tribune category. There is no evidence of electors using the Internet in such a way that would enable MPs to have a clear view of what their constituents thought.

The data we have thus tend to bear out the saliency of the party model. MPs recognise the value of having a website, but they utilise it primarily for the purpose of disseminating material about themselves: what they are doing in Parliament and what they are doing for the constituency. It reinforces what they are already doing and seeks to bolster their position and that of their party. It is, in essence, an aid for getting re-elected at the next General Election under the party's banner.

THE INSTITUTIONAL ROLE

If the Internet is to be utilised in an innovative way, the greatest potential appears to be at the institutional level. As we have seen, the UK Parliament has started to organise itself in such a way as to have a cohesive approach to Internet provision. It is also starting to use the Internet in an innovative way, though it is still at a fairly nascent stage in doing so. Parliament has created a unified body for dealing with ICT – the first time a parliamentary department, as opposed to an agency of one of the Houses, has been created – and has begun to enhance its use of the Internet. The Parliament website was redesigned in 2006, and upgrading is a continuing process. It was reconfigured in a way designed to be more user-friendly, geared more to the needs of the visitor than to the institutional structure of Parliament. It includes video and audio coverage of parliamentary debates.

However, the most innovative use of the Internet has been in the use of online consultation. Committees especially have made use of online forums. The Joint Committee on the Draft Communications Bill in the 2001–2 session, for example, used one and reported: 'Taken as a whole, we feel the innovative features of our inquiry such as the online forum have enhanced the openness of our deliberations. We are particularly pleased that nearly 400 people registered for the forum.'[31] Online consultations have also taken place on family tax credit, electronic democracy, the Constitutional Reform Bill, hate crimes in Northern Ireland, connecting Parliament with the public and, via the Parliamentary Office of Science and Technology (POST), on flood management. Perhaps most noteworthy is the use made of online consultation by the all-party group on domestic violence. This helped encourage input from those who otherwise might not have been willing to take part in a parliamentary inquiry.[32]

By 2004, Professor Stephen Coleman was able to tell the Modernisation Committee of the House of Commons that: 'On-line consultations are something that you [Parliament] have in fact pioneered, and have done better than any other parliament in the world. There is quite a lot of data suggesting that these consultations have had an effect on the fairly small minority of people who engaged in them'.[33] Those likely to be interested in particular parliamentary inquiries are generally small in number but, by exploiting the Internet, parliamentary committees have the capacity to reach those who may not previously have thought of engaging with their work. The potential of such consultation was recognised by the Constitution Committee of the House of Lords in its examination of the ways in which Parliament's role in the legislative process could be strengthened: it recommended the greater use of e-consultation, seeing it as 'one of the tools available to parliamentary committees to consult the public and interested groups.'[34]

Parliament has thus made use of the Internet in a way that is somewhat more innovative than the use made of it by most MPs. Having developed a co-ordinated approach at rather a late stage in Internet usage, it has made up for some lost time. More resources are being devoted to the website and there is much more that it could do to exploit the Internet. It could, for example, permit online petitions (10 Downing Street has an e-petition site) as well as develop the interactive capacity of its website.

CONCLUSION

The use that is made of the Internet by MPs is in line with expectations. The model that fits best with the use made of the Internet by MPs is the party model. MPs use it to promote their own cause and that of their parties, essentially as an extension of what they already do: it is used as a medium for making speeches, press releases and details of the MPs' activities available to constituents. Few MPs reject it, or seek to use it to bolster an independent status or to discover the collective views of their constituents. Perhaps for those reasons relatively few people appear to be interested in Members' websites. Although a plurality of respondents to one survey said that the Internet would be their first source to find information about the local MP,[35] another found that of those with access to the Internet, only two per cent had visited an MP's website in the previous 12 months.[36] This compares with five per cent who had visited the Parliament website.

The greatest potential for innovative use of the Internet is by Parliament at the institutional level. There has previously been little opportunity to promote the institution to the public. That has changed with the televising of proceedings and the development of the Internet. Both Houses have appointed information officers, and the institutional structures have been reformed in order to enhance the institution's use of the Internet. The website provides a central accessible source for information about Parliament and what it discusses. There is also scope for using it by the different agencies of each House. Electors may be able to find out as much about what their MP is doing through the Parliament website as through the MP's own website. Developing the website may also be a means of disseminating information about the institution and its members, in a way that does not prove controversial. Devoting public money to MPs' own websites has not necessarily proved popular. In March 2007, MPs voted for each Member to have an annual £10,000 'communications allowance', essentially to help develop their websites. To critics, it was seen as a means of giving incumbents an unfair advantage. The action taken by the House could be seen as rational from the point of MPs keen to be reelected, but in terms of popular perception it may not have done the institution any favour.

NOTES

1. Following the works of Bagehot and Packenham, these can include educating, problem solving, advocacy, legislative scrutiny, administrative oversight, approving, and acting as a recipient of the views of electors. W. Bagehot, *The English Constitution* (London: Chapman and Hall, 1867). R. Packenham, 'Legislatures and Political Development', in A. Kornberg and L. D. Musolf (eds.), *Legislatures in Developmental Perspective* (Durham, NC: Duke University Press, 1970).
2. P. Norton, 'Parliament Since 1945: A More Open Institution?' *Contemporary Record*, 5/2 (1991), pp. 217–34.
3. P. Norton, *Parliament in British Politics* (London: Palgrave Macmillan, 2005), Ch.9.
4. See R. Ware, 'A New Joint Department at Westminster', *The Table*, 74 (2006) pp. 22–34.
5. Data on IT equipment and spend supplied by the House of Commons to Richard Kendall under a Freedom of Information request, August 2006. I am grateful to Richard Kendall for these data.
6. C. Di Gennaro and W. Dutton, 'The Internet and the Public; Online and Offline Political Participation in the United Kingdom', *Parliamentary Affairs*, 59/2 (2006), p. 301.

7. T. Zittel, 'Political Representation in the Networked Society: The Americanisation of European Systems of Responsible Party Government', *The Journal of Legislative Studies*, 9/3 (2003), pp. 32–53.
8. Zittel, 'Political Representation in the Networked Society', p. 50.
9. D. Judge, 'Representation in Westminster in the 1990s: The Ghost of Edmund Burke', *The Journal of Legislative Studies*, 5/1 (1999), pp. 25–8.
10. Judge, 'Representation Westminster in the 1990s', p. 28. In the event, they opted for the lobby fodder option.
11. See S. Coleman, *Direct representation: towards conversational democracy* (London: Institute for Public Policy Research, 1996).
12. P. Norton and D. M. Wood, *Back from Westminster* (Lexington, KY: University of Kentucky Press, 1993).
13. Hansard Society, *Democracy Online: What Do We Want From MPs' Web Sites* (London: Hansard Society, 2001).
14. S. Coleman, *Technology: Enhancing Representative Democracy in UK?* (London: Hansard Society, 2002). S. Coleman and J. Spiller, 'Exploring New Media Effects on Representative Democracy', *The Journal of Legislative Studies*, 9/3 (2003), pp. 1–16. S. Coleman and B. Nathanson, *Learning to Live with the Internet*, EPRI Knowledge, available at www.epri.org/epriknowledge/contents/7thconference_mat/20050606_1stEPRI_workshop_Backgroundreading.pdf. See also S. Coleman, J. Taylor and W. Van De Donk (eds.), *Parliament in the Age of the Internet* (Oxford: Oxford University Press, 1999).
15. S. Ward and W. Lusoli, '"From Weird to Wired": MPs, the Internet and Representative Politics in the UK', *The Journal of Legislative Studies*, 11/1 (2005), pp. 57–81. W. Lusoli, S. Ward and R. Gibson, '(Re)connecting Politics? Parliament, the Public and the Internet', *Parliamentary Affairs*, 59/1 (2006), pp. 24–42.
16. N. Jackson, 'MPs and Web Technologies: An Untapped Opportunity', *Journal of Public Affairs*, 3/2 (2003), pp. 124–37. N. Jackson, 'An MP's Role in the Internet Era – the Impact of E-newsletters', *The Journal of Legislative Studies*, 12/2 (2006), pp. 223–42.
17. Dod's is an annual compendium of the biographies of MPs and peers and is a staple reference work for anyone wanting to know about Members of either House. For the purpose of our analysis, we have utilised Dod's *Westminster Contacts*, Summer 2006.
18. Information Committee, House of Commons, *Digital Technology: Working for Parliament and the Public*, First Report, Session 2001–02, HC 1065, p. 9.
19. See P. Norton and D. M. Wood, *Back from Westminster*.
20. Norton, *Parliament in British Politics*, p. 235.
21. M. Francoli and S. Ward, '21st Century Soapboxes? MPs and their Blogs', paper presented at the Political Studies Association annual conference, University of Bath, April 2007, p. 7.
22. Francoli and Ward, '21st Century Soapboxes? MPs and their Blogs', p. 9.
23. Francoli and Ward, '21st Century Soapboxes? MPs and their Blogs', p. 9.
24. S. Etherington, Foreword, *Weblogs – a powerful voice for campaigns?* (London: Crisis/Hansard Society, 2005), p. 2.
25. P. Norton, *Dissension in the House of Commons 1945–74* (London: Macmillan, 1975), P. Norton, *Conservative Dissidents* (London: Temple Smith, 1978), P. Norton, *Dissension in the House of Commons 1974–1979* (Oxford: Clarendon Press, 1980), P. Cowley, *Revolts and Rebellions* (London: Politico's, 2002), and P. Cowley, *The Rebels* (London: Politico's, 2005).
26. The data are taken from P. Cowley and M. Stuart, *Dissension in the Parliamentary Labour Party, 2005–2006. A Data Handbook*, available at www.revolts.co..uk
27. S. Ward and W. Lusoli, '"From Weird to Wired": MPs, the Internet and Representative Politics in the UK', p. 73.
28. Francoli and Ward, '21st Century Soapboxes? MPs and their Blogs', p. 8.
29. http://www.davidmiliband.defra.gov.uk/blogs/ministerial_blog/default.aspx
30. www.boris-johnson.com
31. Joint Committee on the Draft Communications Bill, *Report of the Committee on the Draft Communications Bill*, Session 2001-2, HC 876, HL Paper 169, annex 5.

32. Norton, *Parliament in British Politics*, p. 235.
33. Select Committee on the Modernisation of the House of Commons, *Connecting Parliament with the Public*, First Report, Session 2003–4, HC 368, pp. 20–21.
34. Select Committee on the Constitution, House of Lords, *Parliament and the Legislative Process*, Fourteenth Report, Session 2003–04, HL Paper 173-I, para. 213.
35. Coleman and Spiller, 'Exploring New Media Effects on Representative Democracy', p. 9.
36. S. Ward and R. Gibson, 'Virtual Representation and Parliaments, MPs and the Public in the Internet Age', Paper presented at the Centre for Legislative Studies, University of Hull, April 2007, p. 6. See also Di Gennaro and Dutton, 'The Internet and the Public; Online and Offline Political Participation in the United Kingdom'.

Prospects and Concerns of e-Democracy at the European Parliament

XIUDIAN DAI

Whether or not one agrees with the potential of e-Democracy, the Internet as a new tool for political communication is already used in many ways. In Europe, parliaments, political parties and a growing number of individual politicians have already jumped onto the bandwagon of the Internet revolution. Although some writers have attempted to address the many ethical issues raised by the development of cyberspace in general,[1] little has been said about the ethical implications of the Internet for parliamentary democracy. The aim of this article is to investigate the impact of the Internet upon representative democracy through a case study of the European Parliament (EP). More specifically, this paper addresses a number of inter-related questions. First, to what extent and in what ways do Members of the European Parliament (MEPs) endorse, in principle, the use of the Internet for parliamentary communication? Second, is the Internet a trustworthy medium for improving efficiency, transparency and accountability in the twenty-first century parliamentary politics in the European Union (EU)? Third, how has the EP responded to the opportunities and challenges brought by the Internet for improving parliamentary democracy in the EU?

In order to seek answers to the above questions, a variety of empirical data derived from face-to-face interviews with MEPs and parliamentary staff, a questionnaire survey with MEPs and content analysis of the EP website are used. We discuss the EP's institutional provision and promotion of information and communications technologies (ICTs) since the 1990s, before analysing the extent to which MEPs endorse the Internet as a tool for parliamentary communication. We then provide a reality check regarding MEPs' willingness to take advantage of the interactive features the Internet offers. A number of important challenges posed by Internet-based communications are highlighted.

PREPARING FOR E-DEMOCRACY: ICTS AT THE EUROPEAN PARLIAMENT

It is often argued that, if the private sector can embrace the ICT revolution, so can parliamentarians. There is no reason why new technologies should not be introduced immediately in order to improve the responsiveness and efficiency of transactions between government and elected politicians, elected politicians and their constituents, public services and the citizen.[2] To the EP, ICTs have already become an important dimension of its communication policy. Prior to the arrival of the Internet, various videotext systems were used in a number of European countries, such as France, the UK, Germany and the Benelux countries. The EP also deployed a videotext system, which could be accessed from EU member states, where a videotext system is available.[3] Email first appeared at the EP in 1991 as a side function of WordPerfect, which was the official word processing package. As a new medium of communication, the Internet has the technical potential for the Parliament to reach a large number of people at relatively low cost. This prompted the EP to integrate the Internet into its information and communication policy in the early 1990s and a political decision was reached to create a parliamentary Internet server in 1996.[4] Supported by the parliamentary server, email as a new service was officially made available to all MEPs in 1997, when the EP's IT Centre was supported by two mainframe computers and six members of staff.

The importance that the EP attaches to the Internet as part of its communication strategy is manifested, symbolically, in the public display of the parliamentary web address – an action that is rarely taken by any other parliament. It is the Parliament's web address, instead of the postal address, that is exhibited on the outside wall of the EP's main building in Brussels. On the ground floor of the Parliament building, in Brussels, there are still hundreds of traditional letter boxes, but they are already complemented, if not yet replaced, by a total of 9,200 officially designated electronic mailboxes – each MEP and each staff member has one. As of 2005, according to the EP, the number of emails sent and received at the Parliament every month reached 13 million, of which 5 million messages are exchanged with the outside world.[5]

With the EU moving towards a strategy of creating an 'eEurope' and developing the so-called 'pan-European eGovernment', the EP recognises that it cannot afford to be a laggard. It decided to make € 4.36 million available, in 2006 alone, for investing in new ICT equipment and infrastructure on its Brussels and Strasbourg sites through the Directorate for Information Technology (DIT) and the ICT maintenance cost is budgeted at € 470,000 per year for 2007 and beyond.[6]

Institutional provision of ICT equipment at the EP can be said to be generous. The EP provides each political Member with up to four PCs (three for use in the Brussels office and one for the Strasbourg office) with three printers. In total the EP provides 12,000 PCs to MEPs and staff. All PCs used by MEPs and staff are replaced every four years. In addition, MEPs also have computers for use at their home constituency office. To assist online file backup, the Parliament allocates each user 500 Mbytes of storage capacity on the internal network. Our interviewees agreed entirely with the point that each MEP has been provided with a wide range of computers and other ICT equipment, which indicates, by default, that the EP encourages its Members to actively to use ICTs, including the Internet, in performing their parliamentary duties.[7] More specifically, the EP provides MEPs with access to a) the Internet (worldwide); b) EU databases; c) Europarl Inside (EP intranet site, connected to the sites of all the Directorates-General and the EP Political Groups); d) Europateam (inter-institutional intranet); e) MEP-Site (the external website for Members, which offers remote worldwide access to the MEP Standard Software Configuration functionalities) and f) Infomep (MEP intranet site, containing information and computer documentation).[8]

With the re-launch of its parliamentary website in September 2006, the EP seems to be making further progress in meeting the EU's regulatory requirement by providing virtually all of its official documents available on the Internet for public access.[9] In an effort to bring EU institutions closer to European citizens, the EP used the slogan '457 million citizens @ one address' to promote its new website. With users broadly categorised into three groups, the general public, European affairs experts and researchers, information provision on the new website is divided into five sections: 'News', 'Parliament', 'Your MEPs', 'Activities' and 'EU Live'. To be sure, the maintenance and updating of a major institutional website such as the EP site can be a major undertaking and would incur considerable resources. Under the 'News' section, the EP is committed constantly to update the general public on the activities going on inside the Parliament. Those who are seeking more detailed background information about a particular topic can browse through the archives under the same section. Dictated by the unique feature of the EP in terms of being a multi-lingual environment, all information provided under this section is made available in all official languages – now 22 in total. The 'Activities' section can be said to be an extension of the 'News' section in the sense that the former presents current topics in more detail. Under 'Activities', visitors can find legislative documents, such as reports, draft resolutions, minutes and verbatim debates. Similar to the 'Parliament' section, the 'Your MEPs' section provides information related to each individual MEP's background, parliamentary responsibilities and parliamentary work.

In comparison, the 'Parliament' and 'EP Live' sections appear to be more dynamic. In addition to providing comprehensive information about the organisational and operational aspects of the EP as an institution, the 'Parliament' section allows users to submit petitions and inquiries online. Through the 'EP Live' section, events such as plenary sessions, committee meetings, hearings and press conferences taking place at the EP are all covered through webstreaming. This offers the users an opportunity to follow up live events taking place at the EP without having to be physically present in Brussels or Strasbourg.

Regardless of whatever technical features the EP's website offers, the effectiveness of such an institutional portal will be judged by the extent to which it can deliver 'e-services' including information services – easy and effective access to information to increase transparency and understanding of EU policies and activities; interactive communication services to facilitate policy consultation and feedback mechanisms; and transaction services, namely, online petition submission and electronic correspondence with the EP.[10] Undoubtedly, the EP's website now constitutes a major part of 'europa' – the EU's official portal, which is fast becoming a centre piece of the Union's political communication strategy for the information age.[11] To help achieve the goals of EP's political communication through the Internet, the EP web team were preoccupied with a number of key issues in re-designing the parliamentary website including, according to an insider,[12] the following:

Political consideration. The new design must increase the visibility of the EP activities – not only to say what the EP is but also what it does. The institutional website should reinforce the fact that the EP legislates and it legislates in time.

Ethical consideration. In order to make the EP transparent it is imperative that all official documents received from other EU institutions and all documents that are produced inside the EP can be accessed and read by the citizens. It is most important that the EP provides online, continued and real-time information and adapts it to a diverse target audience, including citizens, EU experts and journalists.

Strategic consideration. The website should, perhaps most critically and ambitiously, create a stronger link between the EP and European citizens through an institutional website.

To be sure, parliamentary use of the Internet by the EP is a relatively new experience, although this is already having an impact on parliamentary administration and communication. This impact is in part manifested in the EU politics of distance. The EP operates on the basis of internal 'distance'. Parliamentary sessions take place on two sites: Brussels and Strasbourg. Accordingly, MEPs' monthly calendars are split between the two sites, which will necessitate long-distance travel and costs. Adding to this is the EP site in Luxembourg, where a large part of the EP administration is housed. The geographically split nature of the EP is a politically sensitive issue, which could only be changed by political solutions involving the governments of the Member States. In many ways, ICTs have helped overcome or ease some of the problems created by the geographical and institutional distances 'within' the EP. The development of a VPN (Virtual Private Network) infrastructure, for example, has created a virtual internal environment for intra-institutional communication between the different sites. The use of the EP's intranet has provided great convenience for MEPs and staff to access and distribute parliamentary documents irrespective of geographical distance. For citizens' access to information and documents related to the EP, the Internet is also indispensable today. When it comes to the point about MEP-citizens interaction, however, Internet-based communication does not necessarily mean the arrival of direct and instant communication between elected politicians and European citizens.

In addition to the parliamentary web, the Internet can also be used to raise awareness of the EP amongst the general public. Sponsored by the Robert Schuman Foundation and aided by partners such as the EP and MEPs, an online game website 'BeMEP.eu' was set up for the period October 2006 to March 2007 allowing for the international participants to choose and use any of the three game languages: English, French and Polish. By participating in this online game as 'virtual MEPs', participants would need to group themselves into online political groups simulating real Political Groups at the EP. Through a wide range of online activities, for instance, discussion forums, virtual party factions, online voting, creating 'resolutions' and undertaking virtual training sessions, game participants are expected to become more familiar with and enthusiastic about EU parliamentary affairs.[13]

The EP's electronic communication system, however, has its weaknesses. Among others, the limited provision of information to MEPs inside the Parliament chamber is worth mentioning. Up until now, the only information that MEPs could get on their screen when they are sitting in a plenary session is the topic of debate and a list of the names of three speakers – the person who is at that moment speaking and the following two. This is also the only information displayed on the screen to assist MEPs' voting in the Parliament. When an MEP speaks from his or her seat, rather than the stage, eye contact would be lost with the audience because of the huge size of the chamber. For the audience, they might not know who is speaking if they cannot see the person. Those MEPs who are in charge of the Parliaments' ICT matters seemed determined to change this situation: 'We would like to improve this system to allow Members of Parliament to read [on their screen] what actually the text of the amendment is, for example, especially if it was an oral amendment.'[14]

Another area of insufficient development in the EP's ICT network lies in the lack of satisfactory solutions to security concerns. This is particularly the case when the Parliament is dealing with security and defence matters. One MEP commented on this situation with regret:

> That not only requires another security measure, but that will require also entirely different equipment, which will be screened, so you cannot read the contents of your computer from the outside. This is something which we will have to face in a not very distant future, but we do not have it yet. If we want to have classified information we cannot do that *via* our computers.[15]

THE INTERNET AND PARLIAMENTARY COMMUNICATION: MEPs' VIEWS

Institutional promotion of ICTs at the EP since the 1990s has been matched with the largely positive view of MEPs of the benefits that the Internet offers for improving parliamentary democracy.

First, the Internet is believed to be instrumental to parliamentary work. Among those MEPs who responded to our questionnaire,[16] as Table 1 demonstrates, 90 per cent of them confirmed that they were regular users of PCs; 90.3 per cent are regular Internet users; and 95.1 per cent are regular users of email communication. These figures suggest that for the vast majority, who responded to our survey, there is already a high level of reliance upon computers and the Internet in arranging and performing parliamentary duties. For an MEP's office staff, the level of reliance upon the Internet is even higher. When we were at the EP to conduct interviews, MEPs and their office staff who were interviewed expressed a sense of frustration when the EP's computer network

TABLE 1
MEPs' USE OF PCs AND THE INTERNET

Usage	Number of Valid Respondents	Percentage (%)
a) How often do you use a PC?		
Do not use it	1	1.7
Rare use	1	1.7
Occasional use	4	6.7
Regular use	54	90.0
Total	60	100.0
b) How often do you use the Internet?		
Do not use it	1	1.6
Occasional use	5	8.1
Regular use	56	90.3
Total	62	100.0
c) How often do you use email?		
Do not use it	1	1.6
Occasional use	2	3.3
Regular use	58	95.1
Total	61	100.0

was experiencing disruption or running at a very low speed. Some of them said they could not do any work at all due to the problem of the computer network.

With a generally positive perception about the importance of the Internet to parliamentary work, the majority of respondents confirmed that they spend a significant proportion of their working hours on the Internet. More specifically, as Table 2 shows, 43 out of 61 (or 70.5 per cent) of respondents indicated that they use the Internet as a work tool for more than two hours each day and another 17 (or 27.9 per cent) for up to two hours each day. In contrast, only one (or 1.6 per cent) MEP replied that she does not use the Internet for work purposes at all.

TABLE 2
MEPs' DAILY USE OF THE INTERNET AS A WORK TOOL

Usage	Number of Valid Respondents	Percentage (%)
Do not use it	1	1.6
0–2 hours per day	17	27.9
More than 2 hours per day	43	70.5
Total	61	100.0

Secondly, the Internet has become an important medium, through which MEPs keep themselves informed. One MEP spoke highly of the informational role that the Internet plays: 'We have our email address, the intranet and … the webpages of the Commission, of the Parliament and of the Council. … we are able to be updated of all the important files and what is happening.'[17]

Thirdly, the relationship between the Internet and the EP is also demonstrated by the fact that the Internet has now become an important tool for parliamentary communication. For some MEPs the use of PCs and the Internet is already a preferred way of communication. Claiming to be a heavy user of the Internet, one MEP asserted that the Internet is critically important to parliamentary communication.

> Despite the huge amount of paper you can see in my office, the computer is very important. What is the most interesting aspect in the use of computer? First of all, we could replace, indeed, a lot of paper by using the internal network…. It is very important, especially in the European Parliament, because you are speaking of a parliament where we work with 20 different languages, so when we needed several years ago to print everything with different colours for each language, it was a nightmare. So it is easier to provide internal information, support documents, studies, agenda, and so on, by the Internet. Connecting [communicating with] everybody is easier with the Internet…. I prefer to use the internal email than a phone call.[18]

Echoing this view, some MEPs confirmed that the EP and its Political Groups have already put into practice electronic distribution of official documents, despite the fact that paper-based communication is still necessary. For the active Internet users, there is a high expectation for moving parliamentary communication away from paper-based to electronic distribution. In particular, the creation of an intranet environment, to which access is restricted to parliamentary staff and parliamentarians, was often cited as a very useful development during our interviews. The Parliament intranet is seen by some MEPs as a new tool for improving the efficiency of parliamentary and Political Groups' work as well as offering convenience and flexibility for accessing parliamentary documents:

> … the European Parliament is communicating primarily through emails, and that applies to the Parliament as such, and the [Political] Group as well, and also the Committees and the plenary sessions, the documents which are connected with those sessions are communicated by email, by intranet. We have intranet in the [Political] Group, we have intranet for the Parliament, and you have a plan of what is going on, which Committee is sitting where, what is on the programme, and

which pieces of legislation will be voted, and all the documents are on intranet. So I prepare myself for the sitting, my assistant is looking at the intranet and sometimes when I need something to study more I print it and I read it on the plane or somewhere, in the hotel, but it is not necessary to print it if I am here, I can do it on the intranet.[19]

Our research shows that many MEPs are not merely ordinary Internet users; rather, they have created their own website. Out of the 62 MEPs who responded to our questionnaire, 51 (or 82.3 per cent) of them said they have a personal website.

When asked what purposes a politician's personal website serves, 96.1 per cent of the MEPs regarded the offering of information about their own work as a relevant, or the most relevant, purpose and only one of them did not agree (see Table 3). Similarly, 94.1 per cent of these MEPs saw online communication with their constituents as a relevant, or the most relevant, purpose of their personal website, with only one respondent not agreeing. Getting feedback online from constituents was seen as a relevant, or the most relevant, purpose of their personal website for 58 per cent of MEPs. One MEP confirmed during an interview that the Internet has offered an effective tool for politicians to communicate with their voters.

TABLE 3
PURPOSE OF MEPs' USE OF THE INTERNET

	Number of Valid Respondents	Percentage (%)	Cumulative Percentage (%)
a) Purpose of website: offering information about own work			
Most relevant	42	82.4	82.4
Relevant	7	13.7	96.1
Fairly relevant	1	2.0	98.0
Not important	1	2.0	100.0
Total	51	100.0	
b) Purpose of website: communicating with constituents			
Most relevant	22	43.1	43.1
Relevant	26	51.0	94.1
Fairly relevant	2	3.9	98.0
Not important	1	2.0	100.0
Total	51	100.0	
c) Purpose of website: getting feedback from constituents			
Most relevant	12	24.0	24.0
Relevant	17	34.0	58.0
Fairly relevant	16	32.0	90.0
Not important	5	10.0	100.0
Total	50	100.0	

> I cannot communicate with all my voters [through conventional means];
> it is impossible. But it is very useful to have a webpage to communicate
> with the voters.... It [the Internet] is easier; it takes not so much
> time than to have it *via* normal mails or phone calls.... It is very,
> very useful.[20]

From the perspective of political communication, the Internet was believed to
be more useful than the traditionally printed media. 'I think it [the Internet] is
much more useful than all the brochures we are printing. For the young
people webpages are much more interesting than brochures.'[21] This MEP has
set up her own website, where she publishes her monthly newsletter as a main
channel to communicate with voters in her home constituency.

The results of our survey also suggest that about two-thirds (66.7 per cent)
of the respondents were already making regular use of the Internet for
disseminating information. A much higher percentage (82.3 per cent) of them
said they use the Internet to search for information.

THE WEAKEST LINK IN E-DEMOCRACY: INTERACTIVITY

It is argued that the cause of voter apathy is not because voters do not want
to participate in politics but because the current system of political
representation is flawed and the interactive nature of Internet technologies
could help reinvigorate the democratic process.[22] Despite the predominantly
positive view of MEPs over the potential of the Internet to assist parliamentary
work and parliamentary communication, the extent to which they make active
use of this new media is rather limited. An interesting indicator of this point is
the use of hyperlinks.

Our study of the EP website in February 2005 indicates that over two-
thirds (502 or 68.6 per cent) of the 732 MEPs did not have any hyperlinks
from their personal profile page of the EP website to an external website –
either a website of their own or one of their Political Group/Party (see
Table 4). It is worth noting that the number of MEPs without any hyperlinks
between their profile page on the EP website and external websites has reduced
recently. Within one and half years since our first web survey in February
2005 the number of MEPs without such links dropped to less than half (362
or 49.5 per cent, out of a total of 731 MEPs) by August 2006. While we
recognise the possibility that more MEPs might decide to create hyperlinks
between their official profile page on the EP website with external websites in
the years to come, it remains a concern that nearly half of MEPs have not
made effective use of hyperlinks, which represent a powerful feature of the
Internet. In the absence of hyperlinks, visitors to an MEP's profile page

TABLE 4
MEPs' USE OF HYPERLINKS

	Number of MEPs	Percentage (%)
February 2005 Survey		
With a hyperlink to own website	192	26.2
With a hyperlink to party website	26	3.6
With hyperlinks to both websites	12	1.6
No hyperlinks	502	68.6
Total	732	100.0
August 2006 Survey		
With a hyperlink to own website	297	40.6
With a hyperlink to party website	53	7.3
With hyperlinks to both websites	19	2.6
No hyperlinks	362	49.5
Total	731	100.0

might not be able to find any further information about their European representative.[23]

When the MEPs' country of origin is analysed, it is not necessarily the case that MEPs from the new Member States have a lower level of usage of hyperlinks. On the contrary, as of August 2006, Slovenia was the only Member State where all of its seven MEPs were found to have hyperlinks linking their personal profile page on the EP website with external websites. This suggests a very high level of effective usage of the interactive features of the Internet. In contrast, Luxembourg and Estonia were at the bottom of the list with 83.3 per cent of their MEPs without any hyperlinks to external websites. In between these two extremes are countries such as Portugal, the UK and Sweden, where 66.7 per cent, 50 per cent and 36.8 per cent of their MEPs, respectively, were found not to have made any use of hyperlinks on their EP profile page. These figures indicate that a clear divide does not exist between the old and new Member States within the EU in terms of MEPs' use of hyperlinks on their personal page of the EP website.

When MEPs' political orientations are analysed, we found that, although MEPs in the Groups of Greens/European Free Alliance came on top, in terms of having hyperlinks on their personal profile page, it is MEPs from the largest or larger political groups that tended to have a higher level of hyperlink usage. More specifically, 48.9 per cent, 45.7 per cent and 44.9 per cent of MEPs from the European People's Party, the Socialist Group and the Group of the Alliance of Liberals and Democrats, respectively, had no hyperlinks with external websites on their EP personal webpage. In comparison, higher percentages of MEPs belonging to the smaller political groups such as the Confederal Group of the European United Left-Nordic Green (61 per cent), Union for Europe of the Nation Group (50 per cent), Independence/Democracy Group (79.3 per cent) and Non-attached Members (56.8 per cent) did not have hyperlinks on their profile page on the EP website. Therefore, it is not necessarily the case that smaller political parties or political groups would make more active use of the Internet than their larger counterparts.

CHALLENGES OF E-DEMOCRACY

There are many advantages associated with Internet-based communication. However, cyberspace is not a problem-free zone. In fact, the EP and MEPs are faced with a plethora of ethical dilemmas, which pose a significant challenge to active users of Internet-based communications and help explain, at least in part, why some politicians are reluctant to go online. MEPs are provided with access to hardware, software and network. However, they are not provided with the necessary policy solutions to cope with the various ethical issues raised by the use of the Internet.

Transparency vs. Security

The lack of confidence in online security serves as a major barrier to the development of e-Democracy. In addition to legitimate use of the Internet, there is also malicious information and communication generated in cyberspace. The European Commission has identified a number of security threats to information systems including a) hacking – unauthorised access to information systems; b) denial of service attack – disruption of information systems; c) computer viruses – malicious software that modifies or destroys data; d) sniffing – interception of communications and e) 'spoofing' or identity theft.[24] Because these actions would hinder or interrupt the functioning of and access to an information system, they are deemed to be punishable under national and international law.[25]

The Internet allows different types of communications equipment to be connected to it and exchange data between each other. So far as the EP's operation is concerned, MEPs now represent citizens of 27 Member States with 22 official languages, which would demand a large number of linguistic varieties for computer software. In addition, MEPs work across at least three main geographical sites: the EP in Brussels, the EP in Strasbourg and their home constituency. There is no doubt that compatibility between different communication terminals and multi-site connectivity is essential to ensure the smooth operation of the EP and MEPs.[26]

Another side of the same coin is that network security is becoming an increasing challenge for the EP's ICT team. Although the EP was able to implement measures to improve the level of security for its intranet (the internal communications infrastructure), it does not have much control over the security of the global Internet and the various types of communications devices MEPs use. For this reason, the EP has the following guidelines for MEPs and parliamentary staff:

> Given that this network [Internet] will be usable with equipment whose security Parliament has no control over and that it will provide broad access to the Internet, it will be impossible to guarantee a level of service and security equivalent to that offered by the internal network. Each user will therefore be responsible for the risks and disturbances generated, in particular as regards data security and anti-virus protection.[27]

The EP and MEPs are caught in the contest between the ever-increasing power of Internet communication and the growing risk of malicious cyber attacks. Nearly one-third (32.1 per cent) of our 62 questionnaire respondents regarded the fact that the Internet is not a secure communication tool in terms of privacy as a most significant or significant problem.

In order to improve security in its ICT network, the EP has introduced a standard configuration, which includes Microsoft Windows XP, Microsoft Office suite, Microsoft Outlook, Microsoft Internet Explorer, Dreamweaver (web authoring tool), FTP Voyager (for file transfer *via* the Internet), Rightfax (a computer fax tool), Acrobat Reader and McAfee (Anti-virus software). Other than these software packages, MEPs are not allowed to add any additional software and their Local Support Unit (LSU) comprises the only authorised people to install, modify or upgrade the software configuration of EP workstations for reasons such as 'an unchecked file or program from outside may transmit a virus to the workstation and subsequently to the EP network'.[28]

Who Should Fund an MEP's Personal Website?

The fact that on the EP website each MEP is offered only one personal profile page has prompted some MEPs to develop their own website independent of the EP site. The creation, updating and hosting of a website are often done at a cost. Who should pay for an MEP's personal website – the EP, the political groups or MEPs themselves?

The EP funds the creation of, and allocates storage space for, the websites of all committees and political groups. But this help does not extend to individual MEPs. Therefore, some MEPs have resorted to the parliamentary allocation, the 3,701 budget, for funding their personal website. This potentially creates a problem: the parliamentary budget may not be used for a political purpose: 'I cannot use it [my website] for electoral campaigns; it is for my daily work; it is for my work as a deputy; but it is not allowed for using in election campaigns.'[29] On a website funded by the parliamentary budget, an MEP can say things such as 'Please go to vote, these elections are important, please participate' but they cannot say 'Please vote for me' or 'Vote for my party'.[30] If websites are important to election campaigns, an alternative to parliamentary budget could be for political groups and/or the affiliated national political parties to fund MEPs' personal websites independent of the European Parliament. However, political groups or parties usually cannot afford this.[31]

Because of the inappropriateness of using a parliamentary budget-funded website for political and electoral campaigns, many MEPs have managed to set up separate websites to fulfil their needs. This has led to the situation of website proliferation including, among others, the co-existence of the EP website, the Parliamentary Committees' websites, Political Groups' websites and the MEPs' personal websites. Although each of these websites tends to serve a unique purpose, they are, as sources of information, competing for public attention. One MEP agreed that the creation of multiple websites 'is a little bit confusing for the outside [world]'.[32] This situation is exacerbated by MEPs' inactive use of hyperlinks – visitors to the EP's website might not be able to jump onto an MEP's other website(s) from his or her personal profile page, unless the visitor is an experienced Internet user who knows how to find information on the Internet through, for example, search engines.

Institutional Codes of Conduct

Another interesting finding in our study is that none of our MEP interviewees was aware of any parliamentary codes of conduct, which could help them better cope with the various ethical challenges they experience in using the Internet for parliamentary communication. Such issues as who should answer the emails sent to an MEP, which categories of emails should be answered and how quickly the emails should be answered or acknowledged have not been addressed in any institutional policy. One MEP frankly confirmed that 'I am not sure if we have been provided with a code of conduct'.[33] The reason why the EP has yet to implement any sort of code of conduct could be explained in part by the lack of political will and technical expertise:

> My impression is that from all the deputies who are politically responsible, only a small part can really handle the issue of Internet and email and so on, they have not enough technical knowledge...we even have deputies who do not work at all with the computer and emails.[34]

As far as institutional responsibilities are concerned, some MEPs acknowledged that the issue of how to deal with the flow of information is not something that the EP currently deals with.[35] To a certain extent, the EP is caught in between an established legal framework and the dynamic of technical changes:

But the problem is that you have certain forms of official communications which are legally binding;…they have to send this by post. It is not possible to send it by email, because it is written in the law, so they have to follow the legal basis, and there are many such legal procedures that are done by post, so you have to do it by post.…at the moment the space to use email communication is somehow legally restricted for official communication. But it is gradually expanding, and I think it will expand in the future.[36]

In the absence of clearly defined institutional codes of conduct, many MEPs remain wary of the value of Internet-based communication. In rating the issue of emails' inability to bear signatures or attach official documents, 41.1 per cent of the 56 MEP respondents regarded this as a significant, or most significant, problem. With an increasing number of citizens becoming used to electronic communications, law makers in Europe might one day have to look into the changed, and still changing, world of communication with a view to making digitally transmitted official documents as authoritative as their hard copy equivalents.

We found during our research that the issue of whether the EP should have an institutional code of conduct with regard to Members' use of the Internet has emerged as an important topic in parliamentary debate, although no resolution has been reached.

'This is discussed in the meetings of the Vice-Presidents of the parliament. They are discussing that, and then they inform the [Political] Groups. It is more a question of the Vice-Presidents and the [Political] Groups.'[37]

Undoubtedly, the ethical dimension of the parliamentarians' use of the Internet is not being treated lightly at the EP. A challenge ahead for the EP, however, is to reach an institutional and political consensus over a technically very complicated and fast evolving issue.

CONCLUSION

Research findings presented in this article suggest that the Internet revolution is fast becoming embedded in the European Parliament as a new tool for parliamentary communication. As an institution, the EP has made significant progress in improving its internal communications infrastructure and deploying ICT equipment in the offices of its political Members and staff. The EP has also promoted the development of a major institutional web portal for online information provision to keep the general public informed of its activities. Meanwhile, the results of our questionnaire survey and face-to-face interviews seem to indicate a generally very positive view of the MEPs towards the Internet. Most MEPs who participated in our survey claimed to be active users of the Internet in their work. They also expressed a very positive attitude towards the use of the Internet as an important element of their political communication strategy because of the Internet's many advantages. ICTs in general, and the Internet in particular, have already generated a positive impact on parliamentary administration and communication at the EP by helping overcome the problems associated with internal geographical distances and institutional boundaries, thus improving efficiency.

Online information access has, to a great extent, reduced the distance between European citizens and the EP. However, the EP's reluctance in making use of online interaction with citizens does suggest that e-Democracy at the EP remains largely a one-way traffic – citizen's online petition and inquiries were answered by conventional post, at best.

Development of e-Democracy at the EP is further hindered by a plethora of challenges. First of all, MEPs are faced with a growing level of online insecurity. While this technical issue was regarded as one of the main concerns among those Internet users at the EP, it might also serve as a legitimate excuse for those MEPs who prefer staying off-line. Secondly, the issue of who should finance the creation and maintenance of MEPs' personal websites begs further consideration. Under normal circumstances, MEPs are not expected to use their parliamentary budget-funded website to assist their electoral campaign. This might lead to proliferation of personal websites related to parliamentary and political communication. It seems desirable for the EP, political groups, parliamentary committees and MEPs to adopt a strategic approach towards the funding of MEPs' personal websites so that parliamentarians do not have to diversify their financial resources and time in maintaining multiple websites. The public would then also be able to access information on any MEP through a single website. Finally, the absence of appropriate and adequate institutional codes of conduct to guide parliamentarians' use of the Internet was not helpful. Until this policy gap is closed, we are reminded that 'all jobs are conducted within structures and if the structure does not adapt to accommodate new technologies there is no point in blaming those trapped within it'.[38]

In contrast to the EP's institutional promotion and MEPs' positive perception over the potential of the Internet to assist the democratic process, we found that a significantly high number of elected politicians at the EP could not be said to be active users of the Internet. This was demonstrated by the failure of a large number of MEPs to make effective use of hyperlinks between their profile page on the EP site and externally maintained websites. The fact that MEPs from some new Member States have used hyperlinks more actively than those from economically more advanced EU countries suggests that the issue of digital divide was not as significant as it might have been perceived in the EU context. Moreover, MEPs from smaller political groups seemed to be less active than those from the larger political groups in using hyperlinks. On the whole, the poor use of the interactive elements of the Internet suggests that the development of e-Democracy at the EP is only at a very early stage.

NOTES

1. For example, C. J. Hamelink, *The Ethics of Cyberspace*, (London: Sage, 2000).
2. Lord Freeman, *Democracy in the Digital Age*, (London: Demos, 1997).
3. Interview with EP staff member responsible for the parliamentary web, Brussels, 28 June 2005.
4. Interview with EP staff member responsible for the parliamentary web, Brussels, 28 June 2005.
5. Figures are quoted in EP, *Strategic Guidelines on Information Technology in the EP*, draft, PE 359.069/BUR (Brussels: EP, 2005). Needless to say, the addition of Bulgaria and Romania to the list of EU Member States since the beginning of 2007 has further increased the number of officially assigned email boxes at the European Parliament.
6. European Parliament, *Strategic Guidelines on Information Technology in the EP*.
7. Interview with Polish MEP, Brussels, 30 June 2005.
8. 'EP standard configuration for the Members', information provided by European Parliament ICT staff member during interview in July 2005. Further telephone interviews conducted by the author on 4 June 2007 with staff at the EP's ICT Local Support Unit in Brussels and the EP Intranet Services Unit of the Directorate Publishing and Distribution in Luxembourg, which is part of Directorate General Translation and Publishing, confirmed that 'Europarl Inside' is the EP's general institution-wide intranet site, to which all staff members and MEPs have access. According to the same interviews, each Directorate General have their own and specialized 'intranet', which is linked to 'Europarl Inside'. The interviewee in Luxembourg revealed that the EP's institutional intranet service will be overhauled by the end of 2007 with a view to making the EP intranet more oriented towards serving the needs of MEPs by providing them with a more individualised information service. 'Europarl Inside' as the EP's institutional intranet is different from the EPADES (European Parliament Administrative Document Exchange System), which is a file exchange system developed for managing the EP's internal work flow. The latter works with a file explorer, which opens documents on EPADES in Word format, and, therefore, does not constitute a web-based system. For further discussion on the use of EPADES by EP committees, see the article by Shahin and Neuhold in this volume.
9. EU regulation requires that each of the three main institutions, the Commission, the Council of Ministers and the Parliament, need to create an online register of its official documents and ensure the majority of their documents are accessible to the public. For details see EU Regulation No 1049/2001 of the EP and of the Council, 'Public Access to European Parliament, Council and Commission Documents', *Official Journal of the European Communities*, L 145/ 43 (Brussels, 31 May 2001).
10. EP, 'Important Legal Notice', http://www.europarl.euroopa.eu/tools/disclaimer/defaut_en.htm (accessed 26 May 2006).
11. For more details about the EU's new communications strategy see European Commission, *White Paper on a European Communication Policy*, COM(2006) 35 final (Brussels, 1 February 2006).
12. Interview with the EP's web team leader, Brussels, 28 June 2005.
13. For details about the 'BeMEP.eu' internet game, see www.bemep.eu.
14. Interview with Polish MEP, Brussels, 30 June 2005.
15. Interview with Polish MEP, Brussels, 30 June 2005.
16. A questionnaire was sent by post to all of the 732 MEPs in 2005 and 62 of them completed and returned the questionnaire.

17. Interview with German MEP, Brussels, 28 June 2005.
18. Interview with Portuguese MEP, Brussels, 30 June 2005
19. Interview with Portuguese MEP, Brussels, 29 June 2005
20. Interview with German MEP, Brussels, 28 June 2005.
21. Interview with German MEP, Brussels, 28 June 2005.
22. K. McCullagh, 'E-Democracy: Potential for Political Revolution?', *International Journal of Law and Information Technology*, 11/2 (2003), pp.149–61.
23. Note that it is not unlikely that some MEPs might have information provided on websites that are independent of and not hyperlinked to the European Parliament website.
24. European Commission, *Network and Information Security: Proposal for a European Policy Approach*, COM(2001) 298 final (Brussels, 6 June 2001).
25. European Commission, *Proposal for a Council Framework Decision on Attacks Against Information Systems*, COM(2002) 173 final (Brussels, 19 April, 2002).
26. The EP's Directorate for Information Technology alone, for example, has the task of supporting approximately 150 kinds of information technology applications, which are used by MEPs and parliamentary staff.
27. EP, *Strategic Guidelines on Information Technology in the EP*, p.4.
28. 'EP Standard Configuration for the Members', undated document provided by EP ICT staff member during interview, July 2005.
29. Interview with German MEP, Brussels, 28 June 2005.
30. Interview with German MEP, Brussels, 28 June 2005.
31. We have not been told by MEPs how much the creation and updating of a personal website would cost them. But one MEP did reveal that one of the two assistants was employed for the purpose of updating her website. This surely accounts for a significant proportion of her 3701 budget.
32. Interview with German MEP, Brussels, 28 June 2005.
33. Interview with Czech Republic MEP, Brussels, 28 June 2005.
34. Interview with German MEP, Brussels, 28 June 2005.
35. Interview with Polish MEP, Brussels, 30 June 2005.
36. Interview with Czech Republic MEP, Brussels, 28 June 2005.
37. Interview with German MEP, Brussels, 28 June 2005.
38. S. Coleman, *Technology: Enhancing Representative Democracy in the UK?* (London: Hansard Society, 2002), p. 26.

'*Connecting Europe*': The Use of 'New' Information and Communication Technologies within European Parliament Standing Committees

JAMAL SHAHIN and CHRISTINE NEUHOLD

Following the logic that 'interests' turn to where the (institutional) 'power' is, the European Commission and the Council of Ministers were the main targets of interest groups until the Single European Act (1987). Since the enlargement of the European Parliament's (EP) role by way of the co-operation and co-decision procedures, the focus has increasingly shifted to this institution. The EP, as the only directly elected EU institution, portrays itself as *the* forum that is open not only to the input of lobby groups but also to that of the 'average' citizen.[1] At the same time, it is almost conventional wisdom that Members of the European Parliament (MEPs) have increasingly been facing the challenge of having to acquire expert knowledge in fulfilling their role as co-legislators and resort to 'new' information and communication technologies (ICTs) in this quest.

Our analysis is rooted within the larger debate of the possible contribution of the Internet, as one of the major developments in ICTs in recent years, in encouraging the development of a European public space, or, public sphere.[2] The focus will be on the more recent work of eDemocracy theorists and practitioners, who highlight many of the challenges that need to be overcome if intending to use the Internet as a communication medium for democratic purposes. This theoretical elaboration will outline the critical points of Internet and other ICT usage by parliamentarians, particularly in the European arena.

By way of empirical analysis of interview data and secondary literature, we will analyse the challenges that the Internet both poses and attempts to solve. The discussion will focus on new technologies in general, the analysis going beyond the use of email by MEPs and also focusing on potentially interactive technologies such as discussion fora and newly emerging Web 2.0 technologies. The analysis is specifically directed towards members of EP committees that are involved within the legislative process, and here the focus is very much on key players within these fora. This choice is based on the fact that members of EP committees are increasingly faced with the challenges of co-decision, that is, having to live up to their role as (co-)legislators. Another factor that is closely linked is the fact that representatives of civil society and interest groups are very much aware of the impact key players in committees such as rapporteurs can have on the policy process and very often contact them directly due to their (temporary) legislative role.

Against this background the question at stake is the following. How do members of EP standing committees use new technologies in order to, on the one hand, fulfil their legislative role and, on the other hand, live up to their function as 'representatives' of citizens' interests? In this quest, it is noteworthy that we examined the ways in which ICTs have had an impact on EP Standing Committees' external and internal communication. The issue of transparency is crucial to this, as well as how and whether these new methods of communication are reflecting a correlation between 'interests' and 'institutional power.' Closely linked is the question of how and to what extent EP committees contribute to the creation of a Parliament that has a positive impact on the European public sphere, through being an institution that promotes debate and discussion about European issues on a European level?

This study builds on 30 semi-structured interviews that have been conducted with MEPs and administrators of the EP Committees and EP General Secretariat within the framework of a project conducted within the Fifth Framework Programme on Research and Development. This is supplemented by further research concerning the communications policy of the EP, particularly its use of the Internet, which has emerged while participating in an EU-funded project, which helped parliamentarians (mainly at the national level) come to terms with the impact of new technologies. Furthermore, interviews have been carried out with members of committees that deal with issues of special salience, as here the assumption is that these MEPs will increasingly be subject to 'outside' input by way of interest groups resorting *inter alia* to ICTs, such as, for example, email or e-petitions.

This study takes the following structure. First, the theoretical debates surrounding Internet use by parliamentarians in a European context are discussed. Next, a focus on the EP's Committees shows how their role has emerged in recent years in order to explore the changed demand for the use of ICTs to improve both external and internal communication within these fora. Subsequently, results of interviews will be highlighted, which show to what extent the communications 'revolution' has actually changed the activities of EP Committees. Finally, conclusions are drawn as to the impact of ICTs on the development of the (democratic) link between EU institutions and citizens.

THEORETICAL ASPECTS OF THE COMMUNICATIONS 'REVOLUTION' FOR MEMBERS OF PARLIAMENT

From the middle of the 1990s onwards, there has been debate surrounding the contribution of new ICTs in curtailing what the OECD has called a 'declining confidence in key public institutions.'[3] The European Parliament has a particular interest in the use of the Internet to connect to European citizens and voters. This is both in terms of using the Internet as a tool for providing information, as well as enabling two-way communication with its 493 million citizens. Without going through an already established and largely discussed debate on the potentials and problems of the use of Internet and other ICTs in parliamentary democracies,[4] several attempts of this debate, with specific reference to the European Parliament, will be made here. This is to show how and why EP Committees were selected as the main unit of analysis. In our conclusions to this paper, we will also aim to relate our insights to the theoretical aspects of the debate.

In a recent paper on the topic of the development of a European Public Sphere, Ruth Wodak and Scott Wright made the case that a discussion forum, established at the European level, and by the European Commission, showed the first signs of a European Public Sphere. It is almost conventional wisdom that this concept of a public sphere dates back to the work of Jürgen Habermas in the 1960s, who defined it as a virtual or imaginary community, which does not necessarily exist in any identifiable space. In its ideal form, the public sphere is 'made up of private people gathered together as a public and articulating the needs of society with the state'.[5]

The paper by Wodak and Wright concluded that, although the discussion forum 'offered considerable potential for reducing the democratic deficit in terms of the nature of the discourse, they are not used by policy-makers in any way.'[6] Although the Internet offers great potential, it is not exploited by policy-makers, in this case Commission officials. This brings the question to the fore whether representatives in EP Standing Committees do in fact make use of the potentials the Internet has to offer.

These theoretical aspects of the debate revolve around several key characteristics of new ICTs, which look to broaden the debate solely from a technological one-to-one concerned with the nature of democracy and democratic activity.[7] These characteristics are: the ability to increase dissemination of information and to provide opportunities for greater interaction (including deliberation) between institutions and also between represented and representative.[8] This can be invoked in different stages of the decision-making process, from agenda setting right the way through to the monitoring process.

First, geography and time provide limits to the amount of work that elected parliamentary representatives can carry out with their constituents. Therefore, geography-independent and asynchronous contact with voters, such as that furnished by the Internet, provide a possible solution to delimiting the physical constraints placed on the parliamentarians. One of the potential downsides of this is that as the barriers to communication with M(E)Ps are reduced, representatives can easily get overwhelmed with irrelevant, repetitive and, simply, too much information. This can limit a representative in their effectiveness in debates, and can require representatives to be experts in all issues discussed by the parliament.

Secondly, new ICTs also provide opportunities for greater transparency, which is one of the main goals of a democratic parliament. One of the downsides of these opportunities is that far more work has to be put into ensuring transparency is provided, which requires additional resources.

Thirdly, new ICTs can encourage – alongside the right institutional incentives and structures – deliberation between participants in a debate through the use of various ICT-based tools.[9] This is in recognition of the fact that a multiplicity of actors are involved in decision-making processes, which do not just include individual citizens (and at the EU level it rarely does), but also lobbying organisations, civil society groups and so-called 'experts', who often participate in helping representatives formulate opinions.

Fourthly, the use of new ICTs can help create a networked mentality in political institutions, which acts to level out hierarchies in working methods and patterns. These technologically managed networks[10] are capable of increasing efficiency in decision-making, but are also expected to enhance the role of networking between different actors.

These four issues described above all contribute to the way in which ICTs could help overcome some of the problems of bridging the gap between European institutions and citizens.[11] It must be stated that the above very brief overview reveals that ICTs provide potentials as well as problems for elected representatives. ICTs are not a 'cure-all' panacea to the problems of engagement with citizens, but they show a potential to facilitate a *rapprochement* between citizens and elected representatives. If global communications have a role to play in reviving democratic governance of existing institutions, it is in enhancing the democratic practice: '[the] ongoing two-way communication between governors and governed.'[12] Until now, however, the focus has been more administrative as organisational pressures to become more efficient in communicating internally have overridden concerns in dealing directly with citizens.

For parliaments, the debates regarding the democratic deficit do provide impulse for change in other ways. The growth of new ICTs and particularly of social networks, through use of Web 2.0 technologies, provides opportunities to revive political institutions. The challenge for MEPs is in learning how to adapt to this new environment. For the EP, these discussions come at a time when it is also reassessing its input into the decision-making process at the European level.[13] Rather than choose to focus on the direct relationship between representatives and citizens, we choose to look at the potentials for opening-up the European decision-making process through EP committees. Throughout the remainder of this paper, the discussion will revolve around the use of the Internet, which includes email, discussion fora and websites by the EP's Standing Committees.

AN OVERVIEW OF THE ROLE OF COMMITTEES AFTER 'MAASTRICHT' (TEU) AND THE CONSEQUENCES FOR MEPS

There are currently 23 committees listed on the European Parliament's website[14] dealing with issues from Agriculture to Women's Rights and Gender Equality. Each Committee has a basic website, providing information regarding meetings, reports and a description of the main responsibilities of the Committee. These sites also contain information on the individual members of the Committees, along with their country and political affiliation. The pages contain links to reports submitted to Parliament by the Committees, which express opinions on issues relevant to the Committee. Committee meetings are held in public, therefore, transparency is not necessarily an issue in this environment. Access to documents created by the Committees is also free, as these are available from the website. They are all given a prominent space on the Parliament's website, yet the task and roles of the committees is not automatically clear to the unenlightened viewer of the site. Furthermore, contact, or interaction, with a committee is provided through a link to an email address to the individual members of the committee. As explored in the article by Xiudian Dai in this special issue, there are various challenges and opportunities that need to be addressed with email communication between citizens and MEPs.

Since the Treaty on the European Union and the (at least partial) upgrading of the EP's role as a co-legislator, EP committees have become a key element in the EU policy-making process and can be seen as a vital contribution to the shaping of legislation – Westlake effectively described them as the 'legislative backbone' of the EP.[15] In particular, the introduction of the co-operation and, shortly afterwards, the co-decision procedure have turned committee chairs and rapporteurs into real 'legislative entrepreneurs', with an external relevance *vis-à-vis* the other European institutions engaged in lawmaking.[16] How has this (re)shaped their perceptions of the responsibilities towards the citizens they represent, and should there be a new way of looking at these Committees from outside the European institutions? The fact that each Committee has a website is already a promising aspect, from the perspective of access to information that has already been produced, but is there the possibility for input into the generation of the Committee's opinions from the average (and interested and motivated) citizen? They have powers, which show that they do actually play a highly important role in the EP's infrastructure, which, thanks to Maastricht and Amsterdam, has increased the power-sharing on a European level.

Formal Powers of EP committees [17]

It is noteworthy that EP committees cannot easily be compared with their national counterparts. In their comparative evaluation of legislative committees' powers, for instance, Mattson and Strøm[18] consider four formal rights[19] that are taken as the core of the committees' purpose. Yet, in the case of the EP committees, either these categories cannot be applied at all or at the cost of a substantial adaptation. First of all, in the context of an institutional setting that does not grant the Parliament the right to propose legislation, the place of committees in initiating legislation is simply not at stake. Secondly, the committees' authority to rewrite bills is heavily constrained by the procedure followed in the specific case: consultation as well as assent procedures, for example, prevent any margin of manoeuvre in amending legislation. Similar limits, again dependent upon the procedure, affect committees' ability to control their timetable (see, for examples, the strict deadlines imposed by the co-decision or budgetary procedures). Also the acquisition of information is still a matter of recurrent disputes between the EU institutions themselves, mainly with the Council, notably in the fields of comitology and foreign policy just to take two examples.[20]

Electronic Tools and Processes in the EP Committees

The institutional, and internal, issues described above can be resolved, in part by ICTs, where knowledge-based systems that enhance the sharing of information can be put in place.[21] Communication and Information Resource Centre Administrator (CIRCA), the EU institutions' Intranet solution, enables documents to be shared between closed groups of individuals. This has been used, in the past, to exchange information between Committees and the Commission, for example.

When committees meet in the two weeks following the plenary session, they prepare the work of the EP. Combining practical and theoretical expertise, they enjoy the formal powers to pose oral questions to the Council and the Commission or to external experts,[22] propose resolutions following statements made by the other Community institutions and propose amendments to the Parliament's plenary agenda. Yet, the most important political powers of the EP committees are connected to the role in the legislative process.

In this respect, first of all, the EP can request to the Commission for legislative proposals[23], which must be based on reports initiated by an EP committee. Email is used for distribution of Commission proposals to various Committees, and CIRCA, described above, is also used to carry out the same task. This is also used to enable the EP committees to provide input into Comitology discussions, to follow up on legislation. Secondly, the Council and the Commission are required to provide information to the EP about their proposals and intentions once a month. Thirdly (and this we identify as the main task in this context), committees then have to draw up reports and opinions on proposals for legislation, which build upon formal consultations of the EP with the Commission and the Council (or on the EP's own initiative).[24] Members of EP committees are, as such, increasingly under pressure, becoming 'policy experts' within a very short time-span. In this context they also rely on 'outside' input, which can be *inter alia* provided by way of new technologies. This is the pivotal point of our investigations–how is the information gathered from the outside, and is there an openness to accept new forms of ICTs as channels for input into the decision making process that is carried out by these Committees and how do these Committees cooperate internally through use of ICTs?

The EP has its own electronic workflow solution, EPADES (European Parliament Administrative Document Exchange System, currently in version 2), which provides a platform for document exchange for parliamentary material, and in particular, the documents to be shared by the committees. This is used to ensure transparency among MEPs and other individuals working in the EP. However, one assistant noted that 'email remains the dominant application in use in the work of the EP committees.'[25] Email is used to distribute the working documents, agendas and amendments proposed to reports submitted to the committees. This must also include the necessary translations. Therefore, email is used as a regular tool for disseminating information between the committee members. According to procedures laid down, documents must be available 48 hours prior to meetings to ensure that time is given to the MEPs to read the documents.[26]

Key Players in Committees

What cannot be stressed enough is the fact that committee proceedings are to a great extent shaped by key players in the committee: committee chairs[27] and rapporteurs, whose role is generally well known, but also drafters of opinion, shadow rapporteurs and committee co-ordinators. The formal officeholders within each committee are its chair and three vice-chairs. The chair presides over the meetings of the committee, speaks for it when discussions preceding sensitive votes are held in plenary and can contribute considerably to shaping legislation. The role of the vice-chair is mainly to stand in for the chair when he/she is not available. Once a committee has decided to draw up a report or an opinion it nominates a rapporteur - when the committee bears primary responsibility, or a draftsman - when it has to give an opinion for another committee.[28]

Apart from the official officeholders, the group co-ordinators can be seen to play a key role. Each political group selects a co-ordinator, who is responsible for allocating tasks to the group members and as such he or she can control the legislative process as it is normally he or she who appoints rapporteurs, shadow rapporteurs or drafts-persons for opinions. The so-called shadow rapporteurs are appointed by opposed political group(s), mainly to monitor the work of the rapporteur.

The Challenge of the TEU and the Consequences for
MEPs as 'Policy Experts'

MEPs who sit on certain committees are required to have a certain amount of expert knowledge on, what are at times, very technical issues. In his research on the 'logic of access to the EP,' Pieter Bouwen identifies this 'access good' of expert knowledge as vital for MEPs when it comes to the expertise and technical know-how required 'from the private sector to understand the market'.[29] From the research we conducted, we found that this 'good' is by no means restricted to the private sector, but also very pertinent within other fields such as the social sector or the policy domain of transport where MEPs are, on the one hand in need of expertise as regards, for example, the legal details of particular dossiers, but also need to be aware of – and try to find a consensus with – actors playing an important role in the field such as trade unions, whose inclusion is crucial in negotiations at the EP level. Our research probed into this aspect of MEPs requiring expert knowledge, on the one hand, and trying to strike a compromise with actors such as trade unions, on the other. In general, the conclusions provided below show that MEPs need to be selective in their information input, and that this is still a one-way process, with little attempt made at electronic interaction or discourse between MEPs and lobbying organisations in preparation for committee meetings.

THE IMPACT OF THE REVALUATION OF THE EP STANDING COMMITTEES ON THE USE OF NEW TECHNOLOGIES BY MEPS

The main question at stake here is whether new technologies can help MEPs in their quest to perform both their legislative and representative role at the committee level. What we mean more specifically is: to what extent are new technologies (and in this context we focused mainly on the use of email) resorted to in order to obtain expert knowledge on the one hand and to include the input of citizens (or those claiming to represent them) on the other? Do these enhance the capacities of the MEPs to make more informed decisions, and then communicate these to their electorate?

Information for discussion at committee meetings is disseminated in several different ways in the EP. There are two internal processes that take place, and one external.

First of all, information is provided to all committee members by email. This information is also available on the Parliament's document exchange system, EPADES. This means that MEPs who are not members of a specific committee can have access to all documents regarding the work of that committee. EPADES is only available to individuals working in the Parliament. At a later stage, all documentation is then provided on the EP's website, and is thus available to the public. Although figures for the usage of these tools are difficult to gather accurately, there is a feeling that these tools are not used by all MEPs. 'Only about 50% of the MEPs actually use EPADES; some don't know how to use it, and some don't want to use it,' was the opinion of one assistant.[30]

In terms of interaction, the story is more complex. There are two specific dimensions to examine here, first of all the internal consistency and interaction between the European institutions, and secondly, interaction with external parties, such as civil society groups and individual citizens. In the first place, we find that all MEPs interviewed concede that new technologies have revolutionised the way they work.

> We use the electronic means of communication a lot. I often wonder how we worked before because it has transformed the way we work. When I first arrived here, we did not even have a fax machine.[31]

This interaction in line with committee-related work, however, is limited to political groups. Generally, little electronic communication takes place between committee members. Interaction is saved for the meetings and/or a formal written procedure of submitting opinions, which requires handwritten signatures on documents.[32]

However positive the impact has been on internal working patterns and processes, the downside is the increased potential for external sources of spam (undesirable, or unsolicited email), among other 'electronic interruptions', which interfere with representatives' roles in the decision-making process. There is little use of new ICTs beyond applications such as email and the EPADES system, which are used to speed up transmission and broaden internal dissemination of documents between Committee members. The use of different applications of new ICTs such as Internet discussion groups is very much the exception than the rule. Only one MEP answered that he had resorted to these tools even if to a very limited extent.

> We have used that only once or twice but we might use that more extensively. Similarly the new generations of laptops, with iChat where you can have more people connected at the same time to the same discussion.[33]

The dominant opinion of MEPs seems to be that MEPs are already overloaded with work, and that to add more channels for communication would not, at the current stage, add value to their work. 'MEPs don't see the advantage of extra, digital, communications channels at the present time,' is the way one MEP's assistant outlined the situation.[34]

Externally, the story is quite bleak as well. Given the need for parliamentarians on these committees to become increasingly 'expert' in the areas of discussion, one could envisage the use of more direct calls for expertise to emerge from the Committees in response to the increased number of opinions they are asked to supply, and given the increasing importance of these committees. Using collaborative tools that are available on the Internet, the so-called Web 2.0 technologies that could create living knowledge-bases or enable discussions on specific topics related to the work of the Committees, would be potentially increasingly useful for the MEPs and their Committees as their workload increases, and thus their need for legitimacy and transparency commensurately grows. However, this has yet to emerge from the EP. The main digital source of information from EU citizens and lobbying organisations from outside the EP remains email.

Departing from this rather commonplace finding that email is one of the main pillars of communication resorted to by MEPs we come to the pertinent question of how these emails are filtered, particularly in the context of EP committee work. Here, all MEPs interviewed concede in the first place that they are constantly 'showered' by email. In this context one must stress that the answers resemble each other regardless of whether the MEPs in question were rapporteurs, group coordinators or drafting an opinion. As one group coordinator put it: 'There is a constant onslaught of mail. It is really not possible to respond to all the mails.'[35] Or as a legal advisor of an MEP pointed out: 'The flood of position papers is huge.'[36]

These position papers are generally sent out by lobbying organisations, specialised in delivering opinions to the MEPs. The use of email by these organisations has multiplied remarkably in recent years. In relation to the discussion on MEPs as experts above, this has been a double-edged sword for their committee-related work. On the one hand, it provides them with information for discussion at the committee meetings, but, on the other hand, this can in many cases be overwhelming. For issues of special salience (particularly of timely topics that are of interest to the MEP personally), MEPs do tend to read as many of these as possible.[37] However, when it comes to position papers on irrelevant or uninteresting topics, these are only (generally) consulted if the source is known to the MEP or his or her assistant.

All MEPs, furthermore, state that it is impossible to answer to all the emails sent and it is interesting to note that regardless of political group or position held by the respective MEPs, a 'filter' is applied in selecting those mails that deserve further scrutiny. This selection is very much based on *who* is behind the message. This is increasingly important in the work of committees as the place, where many issues are discussed in concrete terms in the EP. In recent years, the number of standardised emails sent by citizens to MEPs in relation to their various committee obligations reached, in certain cases, 'thousands'.[38] This overload has caused problems for assistants in the EP, whose task it is to provide the human filter for MEPs' email. While many of these ended up in the MEP's spam mailbox (and were, therefore, deleted immediately), many had to be manually deleted from the mailbox of the MEP. We found that in certain cases, 'filtering is done on a personal basis, particularly when it comes to general subjects.'[39]

One MEP, who is involved in more than one committee, put it pertinently: 'I recognize certain names, certain subject areas and immediately focus my attention on them as deserving a response. There are certain other topics, names or organizations that immediately get trashed. It is only the uncertain ones that are opened for a quick check.'[40]

Another opinion along the same lines reinforced this, and highlighted the specific role of the political group in the MEP's use of email.

> We watch out for certain groups more. This of course depends on the position of the MEP, in the Employment Committee for example the position of trade unions will play a more important role. It is the case

in most committees that not MEPs but assistants pre-select what emails should be answered and which ones not.[41]

And as another MEP put it:

One has to be guided by the question, which interests are at stake here and select by oneself. One tries to ask oneself which citizens and organizations are affected and tries to talk to these.[42]

CONCLUSIONS

The Internet bears great potential for parliamentarians, particularly at the European level, where the development of a public sphere, and thus a way of carrying out representative democracy is clearly apparent. The EP finds itself challenged to position itself within the framework of the European institutions on the one hand, and the European citizenry on the other. Debates on the effectiveness of the EP, given the low levels of turnout in elections, are predominant. The Internet, with its potential to encourage political engagement regardless of political and geographical boundaries, can be seen as one opportunity that European parliamentarians cannot afford to 'miss'. By carrying out a set of interviews, we have shown that there is a lack of embedding new ICTs into the representation activities of those parliamentarians interviewed. This is perhaps, more due to the novelty of the technology, rather than an unwillingness to engage. By looking specifically at Committees in the Parliament, we wanted to see if the focusing of the subject matter, (that is, a focus on issues related to the Committee's work) would see a greater involvement of individual citizens and a broader range of civil society groups, who were perhaps hitherto unknown to parliamentarians. The limited results we have, show that there is little done in the realm of 'opening up,' with many parliamentarians claiming time constraints as limiting the amount of activity that can take place. Some of the questions that are answered by this initial investigation into MEP usage of Internet relating to their Committee work show a few insights that directly inform theoretical insights regarding eDemocracy and use of the Internet in parliaments. These relate mainly to the challenges to enhance online transparency and enable interaction between MEPs and a potential 493 million individuals, not to mention a huge number of interest groups.

First, great attempts have been made to use the Internet as a platform for disseminating information to interested parties and the general public. This is not specifically a phenomenon in the EP alone, but particularly has added value at the European level, where costs of publication and dissemination are likely to be far larger than that of any European public administration.

Secondly, the Internet, as a collection of new technologies, has been used to great impact inside offices, and sometimes, between colleagues. In terms of Committee work, most of the preparation is done electronically, and for this, the MEP's assistant plays a very important role.

Third, regarding the level of connectedness between citizens and Standing Committee members, emails are not always answered; in fact, it has been discovered that some MEPs rely on their knowledge of the networks and participants in the specific policy sphere, and their assistants will often pay scant attention, ignore, or even delete emails that do not come from a known or recognisable source.

It has been shown that new ICTs such as the Internet do provide highly positive opportunities for information dissemination and interaction between MEPs and citizens, including organised forms of civil society. This has the potential, particularly in the case of the EP, to influence the development of a Eur opean Public Sphere. However, in many cases, these opportunities are balanced by human limitations on the amount of information an individual can process. This raises questions of the potentials for interactivity between MEPs and citizens. As in other areas relating to the impact of ICT usage (such as eLearning), one of the major conclusions that can be drawn is that the human element – meaning the usage of – new tools and applications must always be taken into consideration. There must be an appropriate blend between the human element and the technology. Use of technology by parliamentarians to improve their working patterns and procedures, particularly in the internal work of EP Standing Committees has a clear positive gain in many ways. However, broadening this analysis to the use of new ICTs to reduce the so-called democratic deficit does not paint such an optimistic picture.

The argument concerning time constraints raises a highly debatable issue in the use of new ICTs by parliamentarians, which relates to the ethical concerns behind using new technologies to interact with citizens. Discussion on the necessity of a code of conduct relating to use of new technologies is a debated topic, with arguments posed above both for and against.

The limited conclusions we can draw from this first investigation into the role of new ICTs in Standing Committees in the EP show that, several elements of the good governance approach to politics and political activity are being ambitiously followed, particularly in terms of openness and accountability. There is, however, a more fundamental issue of being capable of dealing with the masses of information that the virtual world awaiting parliamentarians presents. Organisationally, there are limits to what can be done within current frameworks, and this inevitably means that parliamentarians often rely on their existing networks to help provide information and opinions. Therefore, while the use of new ICTs has radically changed the role of governments, by enabling them to open up their decision-making procedures and processes to the general public, parliamentarians have a far greater task ahead of them. A possible area of future research should be to investigate in more depth the differences between eGovernment and eDemocracy, and exactly how new technologies can provide more 'representative' and 'effective' parliaments.

NOTES

*Some of the observations of this paper will *inter alia* draw on 30 semi-structured interviews that have been conducted with MEPs and administrators of the EP Committee and EP General Secretariat within the framework of a project 'Governance by Committee, the role of Committees in European policy-making and in policy implementation'. This project was carried out in the framework of the research and technological development programme 'Improving the Human Research Potential and the Socio-Economic Knowledge Base' of the Fifth Framework Programme for Research, Technological Development and Demonstration and financed by the European Community. The duration of the project was from 1 Jan 2000 to 1 Feb 2002. This article is not only supplemented by further interviews with officials concerned with the communications policy of the EP, but further interviews have been carried out with members of committees that deal with issues of special salience.

1. European Parliament, *Lobbying in the European Union: Current Rules and Practices*, Constitutional Affairs Series, Working Paper, (Brussels, 2003), AFCO 104 EN.
2. Of note is the work by Wodak and Wright on the use of the Internet at the European level. See R. Wodak and S. Wright, 'The European Union in Cyberspace: Multilingual Democratic Participation in a virtual public sphere?' *Journal of Language and Politics* 5/2 (2006), pp. 251–75.
3. Organization for Economic Co-operation and Development, *Citizens as Partners: Information, Consultation and Public Participation in Policy-making*. (Paris: OECD, 2001), p. 11.
4. See, for example: C. Alexander and L. Pal, *Digital Democracy – Politics and Policy in the Wired World* (Ontario: Oxford University Press, 1998); B. Barber, 'The New Telecommunications Technology: Endless Frontier or the End of Democracy?' *Constellations* 4/2 (1995), pp. 208–28; D. Barney, *Prometheus Wired: the hope for democracy in the age of network technology* (Chicago: University of Chicago Press, 2000); K. Laudon, *Communications Technology and Democratic Participation*. (New York: Praeger, 1977); R. Tsagarousianou, D. Tambini and C. Bryan, *Cyberdemocracy: Technology, cities and civic networks*. (London: Routledge, 1998).
5. J. Habermas, *The Structural Transformation of the Public Sphere: An Inquiry into a Category of Bourgeois Society*. Translated by T. Burger with F. Lawrence (Cambridge, MA: MIT Press, 1991).
6. Wodak and Wright, 'The European Union in Cyberspace', p. 270.
7. For a broader discussion on these issues, see A. Feenberg, *Questioning Technology* (London: Routledge, 1999), and G. Graham. *The Internet:// a philosophical inquiry* (London: Routledge, 1999).
8. S. Coleman, 'The Transformation of Citizenship?' in B. Axford and R. Huggins (eds.) *New Media and Politics* (London: Sage Publications, 2001) pp. 109–26. See especially pp. 121–3.
9. Coleman, 'The Transformation of Citizenship', pp. 120–21.
10. N. Winn, 'Who Gets What, When, and How? The Contested Conceptual and Disciplinary Nature of Governance and Policy-Making in the European Union' *Politics* 18/2 (1998), pp. 119–32.
11. C. Lord, 'Assessing Democracy in a Contested Polity' *Journal of Common Market Studies* 39/4 (2001), pp. 641–61.

12. P. Hirst, 'Democracy and Governance', in J. Pierre (ed.), *Debating Governance: Authority, Steering and Democracy* (Oxford: Oxford University Press, 2000), pp. 13–35.
13. Particularly in the light of recent Treaty revisions (Maastricht and Amsterdam), and the possibility of a European Constitutional Treaty.
14. See http://www.europarl.europa.eu/activities/expert/committees.do?language¼EN, accessed 3 March 2007.
15. M. Westlake, *A Modern Guide to the European Parliament* (London: Pinter, 1994), p. 191.
16. G. Benedetto, 'Rapporteurs as legislative entrepreneurs: the dynamics of the codecision procedure in Europe's Parliament', *Journal of European Public Policy*,12/1 (2005), pp. 67–88. See also: V. Mamadouh and T. Raunio, 'The Committee System: Powers, Appointments and Report Allocation' *Journal of Common Market Studies*,41/2 (2003), pp. 333–51.
17. C. Neuhold and P. Settembri, 'The Role of European Parliament Committees in the EU Policy-Making Process', in: C. Christiansen and T. Larsson (eds.), *The Role of Committees in the Policy-Process of the European Union: Legislation, Implementation, Deliberation* (Cheltenham: Edward Elgar, 2007)
18. I. Mattson and K. Strøm, 'Parliamentary Committees', in H. Doering (ed.), *Parliaments and Majority Rule in Western Europe*, (New York: St. Martins Press, 1995), p. 285.
19. They select (1) the committee's right to initiate legislation, (2) their authority to rewrite bills, (3) the control of committee timetable and (4) their right to summon witnesses and documents (in order to obtain information).
20. Neuhold and Settembri, 'The Role of European Parliament Committees in the EU PolicyMaking Process'.
21. This, however, is reminscent of the Inter-Institutional Information System (INSIS), proposed in 1979, yet not brought to fruition at the time.
22. Any of the standing committees or subcommittees of the EP may organise a hearing of experts, if it considers this essential to the effective conduct of its work on a particular subject (Rule 151 of the Rules of Procedure). Such hearings may be held in public or in camera.
23. Article 192 TEC.
24. Neuhold and Settembri, 'The Role of European Parliament Committees in the EU PolicyMaking Process'.
25. Interview with Assistant for a Cypriot MEP, 29 May 2007.
26. Interview with Assistant for a Cypriot MEP, 29 May 2007.
27. Each committee has three vice-chairs.
28. R. Corbett, F. Jacobs and M. Shackleton, *The European Parliament* (London: Catermill, 2000), p. 106 and p. 113.
29. P. Bouwen, 'A Theoretical and Empirical Study of Corporate Lobbying the European Parliament', *European Integration Online Papers (EiOP)*, 7/11 (2003), htpp://eiop.or.at/eiop/texte/2003-011a.htm
30. Interview with Assistant for a Cypriot MEP, 29 May 2007.
31. Interview with MEP, 28 June 2006, Brussels.
32. Interview with Assistant for a Cypriot MEP, 15 August 2006.
33. Interview with MEP, 28 June 2006, Brussels.
34. Interview with Assistant for a Cypriot MEP, 15 August 2006.
35. Interview with MEP, 28 June 2006, Brussels.
36. Interview with Legal Advisor of MEP, 28 June 2006, Brussels.
37. Interview with Assistant for a Cypriot MEP, 15 August 2006.
38. Interview with Assistant for a Cypriot MEP, 15 August 2006.
39. Interview with Assistant for a Cypriot MEP, 15 August 2006.
40. Interview with MEP, 28 June 2006, Brussels.
41. Interview with Legal Advisor of MEP, 28 June 2006, Brussels.
42. Interview with MEP, 28 June 2006, Brussels.

Are ICTs Changing Parliamentary Activity in the Portuguese Parliament?

CRISTINA LESTON-BANDEIRA

To what extent are Information and Communication Technologies (ICTs) making a difference to parliamentary work? There is, as already seen in this volume, considerable literature on the way parliamentarians have used ICTs[1] and yet we still know little about the way ICTs are impacting on parliamentary activity. Most of the focus up to now has been on MPs individually considered, rather than the institution of parliament in itself;[2] furthermore, most studies have focused solely on the function of representation, overriding other parliamentary functions and activity. There is also little done on this topic from a legislative studies perspective. And yet, one cannot understand the full extent of the impact of ICTs on parliament without having an adequate understanding of this institution. The way ICTs develop and are used is necessarily dependent on each institution's characteristics. This article incorporates the institution's characteristics in its analysis of the impact of ICTs on parliament, by looking at the case study of the Portuguese parliament.

The article looks at the extent to which the introduction of ICTs has led to changes in parliamentary activity in the Portuguese parliament. It is rather ambitious in its aim to look at the process through which ICTs were introduced to the parliament and how it has been used by staff and MPs. It explains the development of the ICT framework within parliament, as well as looking at MPs' perceptions of these new means, to assess finally the impact ICTs have had on two general areas of parliamentary work: the relationship with citizens and internal processing of parliamentary work. This article is necessarily an introductory piece. Its essential aim is to provide an adequate integration of the ICT dimension in the Portuguese parliament context, so that we can understand the extent to which ICTs have had an impact on parliamentary activity. This is a topic that up to now has only been addressed from an ICT and not from a legislative studies perspective.[3] The article is based on extensive research which includes documentary analysis, questionnaires to MPs, interviews to parliamentary officials and MPs, as well as review of WebPages.[4]

THE DEVELOPMENT OF ICT IN THE PORTUGUESE PARLIAMENT

The Portuguese parliament, the *Assembleia da República* (AR), is a relatively new institution. Although Portugal has had a parliamentary institution since 1822, it is only since 1975 that a democratically elected parliament has been in place on a continuing basis, following the introduction of democracy in 1974. This is therefore a parliament only just coming out of 'adolescence' in a slow process of institutionalisation. ICTs started to be introduced in the mid-1990s, though it is only at the beginning of the new millennium that we see a clear expansion of these new means within parliament. Staff from the Centre for Informatics consider that 1993 was the key year of change – when there was a change of philosophy within parliament towards more open systems.[5] This took place at the same time as the process of reform of parliament – one of the most important moments of procedural change of the Portuguese parliament, identified as an 'opening up of parliament to the outside world'.[6] When asked whether this was a coincidence, a Centre staff member said that there was then a genuine mood from within the institution for change, in particular towards opening up parliament. ICTs were part of that process.

The first parliamentary website (www.parlamento.pt) of the Portuguese parliament was introduced in July 1996 and the first intranet (AR@Net) in 2002, although a networked database on the legislative process was already in place prior to this.[7] Although the introduction of ICTs was rather slow at first, since 2002 we have seen considerable change in this area, namely in pioneering moves such as the solely electronic publication of parliament's official journal and the creation of a parliamentary blogs system – both of which followed the approval of Resolution 68/2003.[8]

Resolution 68/2003 was approved in July 2003 by a unanimous vote from all parliamentary groups (PGs). This Resolution established important stepping stones in the process of expanding the use of ICT in ordinary parliamentary work. The first of these stepping stones was to determine that the AR's official journal, the *Diário da Assembleia da República* (DAR), would be published solely electronically. And so, from September 2003 the Portuguese parliament's verbatim record of plenary debates, the First series of the DAR, has been published only electronically. One year later, the same applied to the Second series of the DAR, where all parliamentary initiatives were published. This means that everything submitted by MPs has to be originally in electronic format or digitised by parliament's services. This is one of the reasons why the Resolution also determined that MPs and PGs should always provide an electronic version of all parliamentary initiatives submitted. Although this is not always regular practice, its formal recognition constituted an important step towards embedding the use of ICTs in regular parliamentary practice in the Portuguese parliament.

Resolution 68/2003 also determined a number of other important steps: that parliament's services should work towards ensuring that documents would be circulated only electronically; that a secure system allowing for the recognition of digital signatures should be developed; that the MPs should be able to access parliament's network from the Plenum's benches; and that efforts should be made towards persuading the Government to use electronic means for the circulation and submission of parliamentary documents. Finally, this Resolution also established that parliament should provide the means for the development of both MPs' personal websites and blogs. The first blogs and personal websites were introduced in May 2004, though with limited use by MPs, as we shall see.

Resolution 68/2003 can therefore be seen as a modern document well ahead of its time and one that signalled a marked change in this area. This Resolution was in great part the direct result of the efforts of one MP, José Magalhães from the PS (Socialist Party)[9] – showing the importance of the role played by so-called *ICT Champions*. MP José Magalhães initiated this bill as well as other similar initiatives, such as the setting up of the first Portuguese PG website, in 1994.[10] Although having a formal Resolution does not imply an automatic embedding of ICT into parliamentary practice, it is an important step towards that process; in particular, the implicit recognition that more material should be circulated electronically and that, eventually, there should be a system of recognition of digital signatures.

THE FRAMEWORK AND SUPPORT FOR THE USE OF ICT IN PARLIAMENT

PGs as Key Mediators

The AR is a heavily party-centred institution where PGs are the main unit of organisation. MPs are elected through a closed list proportional representation system and parties are perceived as the main representative mediator. The more seats a PG has, the more power and resources it has. The mediation of the PG as the main organisational unit is reflected across all parliamentary activity. It is therefore no surprise that the PG plays a key role in the ICT framework and support available to MPs.

Equipment and the main services relating to ICTs are managed by the Centre for Informatics, located centrally at parliament level. However, the Centre has little direct contact with MPs, particularly in the larger PGs. This contact is mediated by technical staff hired by each PG. According to the interviews carried out, each of the two larger PGs (the PS and the PSD) has two of these technical staff and each of the smaller PGs (PCP, CDS, BE and PEV) has one, who often also play other support roles within the PG. These staff are paid from the budget of each PG and so their allegiance is towards the PG in the first instance, whereas the technical staff at the Centre represent parliament as an institution, aiming to provide equal support to all MPs; however, this support is given via the PG intermediary. The PG technical staff are the ones who are in touch with the Centre to relay any needs MPs may have and, likewise, they are the ones explaining to MPs what tools are available, as well as resolving technical difficulties. All interviewed MPs were unanimous in considering the technical support sufficient and of very good quality. Despite the division by PG, the technical support system therefore does work well independently of the PG, at least from an MP's point of view.

The strong compartmentalisation by PG does have other consequences though, in the way ICTs are implemented and used. Parliamentary officials considered this to be one of the main challenges they face in the provision of ICTs in the AR, as the following shows:

(One of the main challenges) is a philosophy that has always existed but that is creating us a few problems in terms of inter-relations between us and the PGs, and that is the PGs' autonomy, which means that they have their own closed systems, there is no hierarchical structure here. This brings added costs and complexity. (...) In terms of the general architecture of the whole system it seems excessively fragmented. It has costs and it brings out some dysfunctionalities.[11]

This compartmentalisation is visible in numerous areas. One clear example is the compartmentalised email systems. Rather than one overall email server and system for all MPs, there is a different email system for each PG.[12] As identified by interviewees, this hinders the efficiency of the services provided and leads to extra costs. It also has consequences on parliamentary activity such as, for example and as pointed out by one MP, the fact that MPs do not have access to the email addresses of MPs from other PGs. Having had previous experience in the European Parliament where MEPs have access to all email addresses, this MP found this particularly frustrating. It also has an impact in the reinforcement of intra-party communication, rather than interparty. Another example lies in the way email addresses are created, that is through the PG representative rather than centrally. As a consequence, email addresses of MPs are not standardised, depending instead on a number of varying rules according to the situation where they were created.[13]

PGs are therefore a key unit to understanding the way ICTs are organised in the AR. Like other resources in parliament, ICTs are distributed according to and through PGs.

ICT Infrastructure and Tools Available

The provision of ICT tools in the Portuguese parliament seems to be adequate. Access to the latest technologies does not seem to be a problem and Portuguese MPs can utilise an array of ICT tools. All MPs have an email address, as well as the possibility of setting up a blog and a personal website, both integrated in the parliament's main website. Thanks to the *Project Mobility*, MPs also have an array of tools that ensures distant access to parliament's networked services. All MPs have a personal computer and all of the MPs interviewed also had a laptop. There is also wireless connection in the Plenary, as well as in many committee rooms. Supporting all of this, the Intranet (AR@Net) gives access to a wide range of documents, as well as services. The new version of the AR@Net launched in 2005 has particularly been commended for its user-friendliness and usefulness. Overall, interviewees were pleased with the tools available.

The inadequacy is to be found instead in the staffing support and working space. Most MPs share an office with at least one other MP and have no personal staff support. Still, today's working conditions do represent a considerable improvement since the 1970s, when MPs did not have any offices. In the late 1980s offices were introduced, shared typically between five or six MPs. But the lack of support staff is particularly patent, especially in terms of research assistance as most of the support provided is for secretarial purposes. Although it varies among PGs, typically each secretary gives administrative support to seven MPs. As for research support, this is given by committee, that is, PGs allocate a member of staff to give research support to their members in each committee; typically, each staff member will support two or more committees. Again this ratio varies among PGs, but it does show the inadequacy of the staff support available to Portuguese MPs. As we shall see below, this has consequences in the way ICTs have been used by MPs.

From Paper to Digital

Another important issue to take into account in terms of what is available in the ICT framework is the extent to which the parliamentary process is dependent on the circulation of paper or the extent to which this process has moved towards digital means – independently of the actual practices and perceptions of parliamentarians. As seen above, the Portuguese parliament does personify pioneering moves such as the now solely online publication of the DAR. However, this is an isolated instance.

There is a growing awareness that documents should be circulated electronically, particularly following Resolution 68/2003. However, in practice this is not always possible. The current regulatory framework requires that any submission of parliamentary work (such as proposals of bills, written questions and so on) needs to be accompanied by a written signature; at the moment this is only possible through handwritten signatures. So, even though some MPs submit their parliamentary work electronically, they also need to submit a printed and signed copy. This is likely to change in the near future though, as explained by the Head of the Centre for Informatics at the Ninth European Parliaments Research Initiative conference.[14]

The Centre for Informatics is currently working on the implementation of a system that will allow the secure and certified recognition of digital signatures, not only within parliament, but also at the other institutions involved in the legislative process (from the President of the Republic to the Constitutional Court). This is at an experimental phase and is due to be implemented in incremental stages. The Centre predicts that systems will be in place before the end of 2007 to allow for the recognition of digital signatures in the legislative process within parliament.[15] Several other administrative processes have recently been digitalised such as the justification of absences. So, this is a time of change for the Portuguese parliament in the digitalisation of crucial processes.

The AR@Net has been an important factor in this move towards more digitalised means. Although the processes may not yet be very digitalised, the amount of digital information available has undoubtedly expanded and this has happened mainly through the AR@Net. The new format of 2005 was designed with the essential aim of making it more user-friendly and becoming the main interface for parliamentary work. It was in this context that the Portal of the MP was created, for instance. This gives key practical information to MPs not only about the institution and its organisation, but also about the job of an MP. This Portal is particularly useful for new MPs. But the AR@Net also includes a wide range of other information from access to the legislative process database to news clips (another feature that is not distributed on paper anymore). By offering such a wide and complex range of information digitally, the AR@Net has led to a higher use of digital means by parliamentary staff and MPs themselves, as we shall see below.

MPs' PERCEPTIONS TOWARDS ICTs

Having established the ICT framework available in the Portuguese parliament, we now look at the MPs' perceptions of these new means of communication and information. Having the ICT means available is an essential step towards embedding ICTs in parliamentary practice, but it is also dependent on the prevailing perceptions, in particular from MPs.

Portuguese MPs are generally receptive to ICTs. Figure 1 gives data from the questionnaires and shows that MPs recognise email as a valued means of communication. It gives the percentage of MPs who agree or disagree with the statement that emails are as important as letters in the way they communicate with citizens and pressure groups. Only 21 per cent of Portuguese MPs think that emails are not as important as letters in their communication with constituents, and an even lower percentage for the communication with pressure groups (six per cent).

This was confirmed by the in-depth interviews where MPs showed a genuine openness and optimism towards ICTs. The importance of these new means was even recognised by the two MPs who we classify as 'ICT beginners',[16] though these did show some suspicion in relation to these means. These two MPs were the only interviewees who considered that emails do not have the same value as a letter, feeling very strongly about this. But, in general, Portuguese MPs felt that the only inadequacies to be

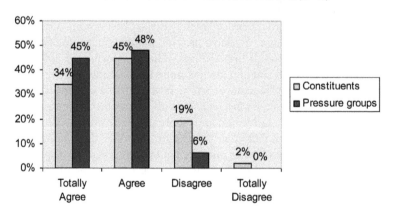

FIGURE 1
IS EMAIL AS IMPORTANT AS LETTERS IN THE WAY YOU COMMUNICATE WITH
CONSTITUENTS AND PRESSURE GROUPS? (N = 47)

found were in terms of how to make the most of the ICTs available, being very hopeful about how ICTs can help them in their job. One MP expressed some worries about security issues, but was nonetheless very receptive to the advantages that ICTs can bring to parliamentary work.

In comparative terms, this reception and openness to ICTs is not as high as in the European or the Swedish parliaments, but it is higher than in the British parliament. Figure 2 gives the average agreement of how important emails are in relation to letters for all four parliaments included in this research. The lower the average values, the more the MPs agreed that emails are as important as letters.

The data from the questionnaires also show, on the other hand, that Portuguese MPs are not as exposed to ICTs as MPs from the other parliaments. Figure 3 shows that Portuguese MPs receive many fewer emails than the

FIGURE 2
AVERAGE AGREEMENT WITH IMPORTANCE OF EMAIL IN RELATION TO LETTER
(ALL FOUR PARLIAMENTS)

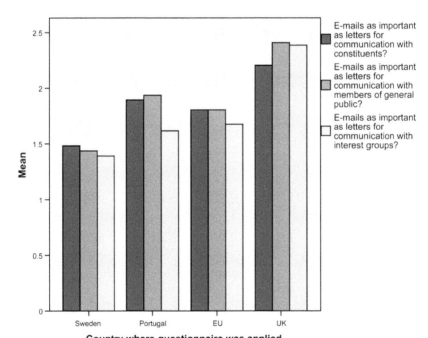

Note: Average of a scale from 1 (totally agree) to 4 (totally disagree). The higher the value, the more MPs tend to disagree with each statement. 'Country' should be read as 'Parliament'. The same applies to the subsequent figures.

MPs from the other parliaments. Most Portuguese MPs said they receive only between 1 and 25 emails per day (57 per cent) and only 19 per cent said they receive more than 50 emails per day. This is in stark contrast with the Swedish MPs, for instance, where 81 per cent of MPs said they receive more than 50 emails per day.

Portuguese MPs, comparatively, also use the Internet far less, as shown by Figure 4. Most of the Portuguese MPs said they used the Internet as a working tool up to two hours a day (62 per cent), whereas the majority of the MPs from the European and Swedish parliaments use it for longer than two hours a day (70 and 63 per cent, respectively).

On the other hand though, no Portuguese MPs said they did not use the Internet (as was the case in the British and the European). Even the 'beginner' MP we interviewed who showed very low levels of ICT awareness thought that he should at least try and use the Internet. And as these MPs lack support staff, many do not have any other alternative but to use ICTs

FIGURE 3
AVERAGE NUMBER OF EMAILS RECEIVED PER DAY (ALL FOUR PARLIAMENTS)

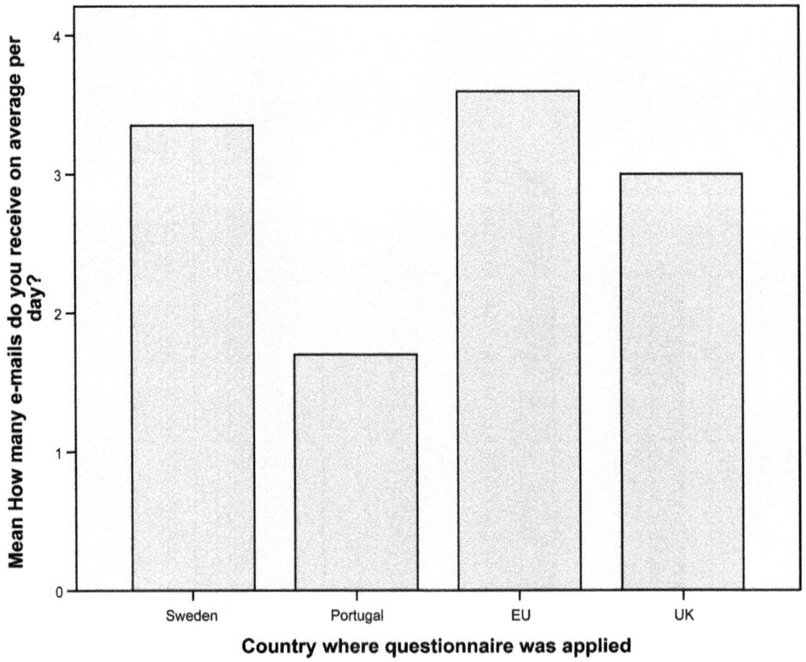

Note: Average of a scale from 0 (no use of email), 1 (1–25), 2 (26–50), 3 (51–100), 4 (101–200), 5 (more than 200).
        The higher the average, the higher the number of emails received per day.

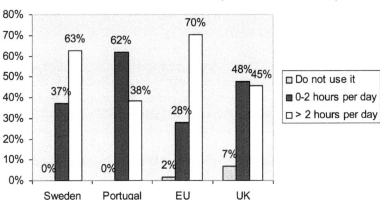

FIGURE 4
USE OF THE INTERNET AS A WORKING TOOL (ALL FOUR PARLIAMENTS)

themselves. The comparative data on the interviews also show that Portuguese MPs have different types of concerns to those of MEPs and Swedish MPs. Whereas Swedish MPs and MEPs emphasised their concerns about email overload and the difficulty in dealing with the circulation of high amounts of information, this was not seen by the Portuguese MPs as a problem. Indeed, up to June 2005 when the interviews were carried out, email overload was still not a problem in the AR. This may partly explain the openness and optimism Portuguese MPs have towards ICTs, but it also shows the lower level of exposure and experience of ICTs. In line with this, Portuguese MPs perceive ICT mainly for its *information* potential, rather than *communication*. This is one of the key differences between the Portuguese MPs and those from the other parliaments included in this research. This is clear in the way they use the Internet essentially for retrieval of information rather than for communication purposes, as shown by the answers to the questionnaires.[17] But overall, the perception of ICTs is an open and optimistic one.

IMPACT OF ICTS ON THE RELATIONSHIP BETWEEN PARLIAMENT AND CITIZENS

The openness in relation to ICTs is particularly clear in the way this has affected the relationship with citizens. The interviews revealed the satisfaction MPs feel in the development of a closer contact with citizens. The AR is characterised by a distant relationship with citizens.[18] In a proportional representation system that puts emphasis on the party as the main unit of representation, a lack of contact between MPs and citizens is to be expected.

This is particularly clear in the Portuguese parliament where the MP mandate is, according to the Constitution, a national one; electoral districts are seen as a mere administrative division of the country, not as 'constituencies' as such. But the Internet has introduced a new channel of opportunities in the relationship with citizens.

All of the MPs we interviewed confirmed that the use of email has led to more people getting in touch with them. Several MPs said that citizens did not really get in touch with them before email. This may well be because most communication would have been directed to the PG instead of the MP. The interviews also confirmed that email is the preferred means of communication by citizens, whereas pressure groups still prefer a more formal type of communication through printed letter. MPs showed interest and satisfaction in this influx of communication from citizens, as the following quotes illustrate:

- 'the use of emails allows to establish relationships between people (...) (and) email encourages communication with us';
- 'I like to communicate with citizens by email';
- 'from citizens we do get quite a few emails (directed personally to me), to compliment what we said or to criticise (...) sometimes they even actually give specific suggestions I think this is when it becomes really interesting and I really like this feedback'.

Several MPs gave examples of specific parliamentary initiatives which were followed up by citizens communicating with them. This would be unlikely to happen if email did not exist, as most printed communication is channelled through the PGs. Even the MP from the PCP (a heavily centralised party) showed great satisfaction in the communication with citizens and gave examples of the way a closer contact with citizens had developed, thanks to email. MPs liked in particular the informality and ease of communication that comes with email. Portuguese MPs tend to answer all emails personally, as they do not have secretarial support for this. They acknowledged that this might not be possible in a few years if the influx of emails increases.

Despite the recognition of the value of ICTs in the relationship with citizens, the web presence of Portuguese MPs is poor. As mentioned above, the AR's website includes a system of personal websites (*PagParl*).[19] However, this facility has only been used by one MP: Mota Amaral, former Speaker of parliament who presided over the approval of Resolution 68/2003; the establishment of his personal website could be seen as setting up an example. As pointed out by staff interviewed, the maintenance of this website is possible thanks to the support given by a secretary.[20] The AR also provides for a parliamentary system of blogs (*BlogAR*), but again the uptake on this has been poor.[21] In April 2007, only five MPs made use of the facilities and, although previously higher, this number has not varied much since it was first introduced in May 2004. Again the so-called *ICT champions* have been the main users of this system, such as José Magalhães or Guilherme Oliveira Martins – both of whom are no longer MPs. The MPs Luis Carloto Marques and Teresa Venda are currently the ones who most assiduously use this blogs system. Despite poor staff support, some MPs do take the time therefore to input information onto these blogs. The blogs are used as a mixture of daily diary and personal website, with the inclusion of comments on current affairs, as well as references to their personal parliamentary activity.

Most of the MPs interviewed did not see any point in having a personal website (or blog). Some of the MPs have had a blog or personal website, but these were created for the strict purposes (and period) of electoral campaigning, usually having the support of their party. Some considered this to be interesting, but said they would not have the means to keep up a website and dismissed the possibility. Only one MP did consider this possibility as a serious one and this was an MP who had previous experience in the European Parliament. Still this MP stated that if they are to maintain a website, then this needs to be accompanied by a reinforcement of staff support. All MPs considered that, in view of the current lack of staff support, it would not be possible to create and maintain a personal website. The main view was instead that they were represented on the web through their PGs' websites. All MPs referred to their PGs as the natural way to provide information to citizens about their parliamentary activity. And indeed each PG has a website, or at least a web presence, which includes information about MPs.

The level of autonomy of the PGs' websites, in relation to their parties, varies considerably, as does the extent of the information they provide about their MPs. All six parties currently represented in parliament have a section dedicated to parliamentary work. Two of these actually have an autonomous webpage for the PG (the BE and the PS)[22] and the other four have a section for parliamentary representation within the party website.[23] The PS website is the PG website that gives the most compre-hensive type of information on the work developed by their MPs and the PEV is the one with the least information. This is to be expected if we take into account that these are, currently, the largest and the smallest PGs. In addition to biographical details, the main information available across all PGs sites, the PS PG website also provides access to the different types of activities developed by MPs (not just the listing of these, but the actual documents or reports), direct access to videoed interventions in parliament, as well as giving general information about the PG's activity. None of these PG websites offer much in terms of web participation, though, beyond giving the email addresses of their MPs (or a form to contact each MP).

Still, special reference should be made to the group of nine PS MPs elected for the district of Braga.[24] This is the only district-based group of MPs, which has a website tailored to its constituency citizens. It is a very recent initiative following on from the 2005 general election, but it is a relatively dynamic site, regularly updated with information about the activity of the PS MPs for Braga. Besides access to the parliamentary activity of these MPs, it also includes a newsletter and a press room, both made specific to the region of Braga. We interviewed one of the MPs from this group, who explained that the site was built, and is uploaded, by a member of staff from the PG, for '*militancy*'.[25] The content of the information uploaded on the site is prepared by all nine MPs, but in particular by one MP who coordinates this work. It will be interesting to see how this unique experience develops.

In parallel with these party-based websites sits the AR's site. The compartmentalisation referred to above is very clear in the way there is virtually no linkage between the AR's main page and the PGs' pages. Although the AR site gives links to each party's site, this is included among many other institutions links in a long list in the *Other Links* section;[26] and note that links are made to each party and not to the PGs. It is as if parliament and PGs acted through parallel channels. Parliament's site looks very static, especially in comparison to those of the PGs, although it does give access to a very wide range of information, from biographical details on each MP to access to parliamentary activity. It also includes a link to AR[tv] – the cable-based parliament TV channel.[27] This allows the viewing of parliamentary debates through the web (live and recorded). The amount of information available on parliament's site is therefore extensive and most of the MPs thought that, as a consequence, the AR is now better known to citizens.

However, the site is not very user-friendly and is cumbersome to navigate (note the lack of integration of navigation bars, for instance). Also, although the site gives access to considerable information, it includes little in terms of online participation. Still, special mention should be made of the online *fora* and petitions. Committees can promote a debate online (an online *forum*), particularly on bills that have to be put forward for public discussion, such as any bill that deals with labour legislation (as determined by the Constitution).[28] The AR site now also allows for the submission of online petitions, though these are individual petitions and do not accommodate the collection of signatures.[29] Although only five online *fora* have been set up, the online petitions have been very popular (though they do not always constitute complete proposals and there is often a repetition of content from petition to petition, differing only in the petitioner's name). The AR's site is currently under reconstruction with a particular focus on its possibilities of 'communication, image and web design';[30] the new version is planned to be available to the public by the end of 2007. The perception that the site needs re-vamping is, therefore, accepted by the institution and is being addressed. The new version should also include a separate webpage tailored for a younger audience.[31]

Although limited, ICTs have had an impact on the relationship between parliament and citizens.[32] Parliament has become a more open and wellknown institution and citizens are getting in touch with their MPs on a variety of matters. MPs find this direct access to citizens particularly gratifying and one notices a clear change in this area. This is shown, for instance, by the PS Braga online experience and the forthcoming reconstruction of parliament's site.

IMPACT OF ICTs ON INTERNAL PARLIAMENTARY WORK

Finally, we turn to the impact of ICTs on internal parliamentary work; the extent to which ICTs have brought changes to parliamentary practice. As seen above, most of the parliamentary processes are not digitalised as yet – though important changes are expected in this area by the end of 2007 including a system of certified recognition of digital signatures. By the time the interviews were undertaken (June 2005), parliamentary work was still heavily reliant on paper; from the summoning of committee meetings to the submission of parliamentary initiatives. Whenever asked about this, interviewees' first reaction was to say: '*it's all by paper*'. There are exceptions and changes in this area though.

Resolution 68/2003 has forced PGs to change their practices and send to the central services electronic versions of all parliamentary initiatives submitted, so that everything is incorporated in the digital DAR. The staff interviewed said this does not always happen (in which case then the central services have to digitalise the material), but it is increasingly done as a matter of practice. What happens in most PGs is that a printed version of each parliamentary initiative is handed in at the Table (where parliamentary initiatives are formally entered) by the proponent MP, but then the respective PG staff also sends an electronic copy of the same document. Many MPs do now submit the original document electronically, but by no means the majority, according to our interviewees; in which case it is usually up to the PG staff to make the document available electronically. Once the new system of certified digital signatures is in place then one would expect an increase in the volume of initiatives submitted and circulated electronically. Still, overall, MPs are using more and more electronic-based information.

The main changes in this area are derived from the Intranet, in particular the new version of 2005. As one of the interviewees from the Centre for Informatics put it, the AR@Net has been an '*engine of change*' in terms of practices. The take-up of the 2005 version was very positive and made MPs start to use more electronic-based information. Very simple examples illustrate this, such as the availability of the Restaurant's Menu in the AR@Net. Three of the seven MPs we interviewed explicitly referred to this as an example of the type of more trivial information they look up in the Intranet. One of those MPs is one of the 'ICT beginners', who explicitly said that he connects to the Intranet first thing when he gets to his office, as a way of finding out what is happening; including '*what's on the Menu*'. Staff from the Centre for Informatics saw this as one of the '*hooks*' used to make MPs utilise the Intranet as a matter of routine in their parliamentary work. Our interviews suggest that this is what has been happening, even with the 'ICT beginner' MPs. Other examples of 'hooks' include useful practical information such as the list of the committee rooms – before now this list used to be circulated to PGs by a porter who went from floor to floor with the list; it is now available in the Intranet.

Another sign of change is taking place at committee level. Although most MPs said that committee documents circulate mainly (if not only) on paper, this does vary considerably from committee to committee. A couple of examples are worth special mention: the Committee on Education, Science and Culture and the Committee on the Budget and Finance.[33] As one of our interviewees explained, when the new Chair of the Committee on Education took over he introduced the rule that no working documents would be circulated on paper; everything would be circulated electronically. Again, as with the Intranet, this procedure has forced MPs to use electronic means more, as this is the only way to access key information for the committee meetings. An interesting instance happened when the committee official said that an MP had justified his absence by email. Could this be accepted? The Chair took the decision that the email was sufficient to explain the absence. Since then this process has become digitalised.

The Committee on the Budget personifies an important step towards a more digitalised process of consideration of bills. This committee made a specific request to the Centre for Informatics for a system that would allow for the digitalisation of the process of consideration of the State Budget. This is a massive bill that parliament considers every year; it is the object of hundreds of amendments and it takes weeks to be considered. This digital system was in place in autumn 2006 for the consideration of the State Budget for 2007: the AR@PLOE. The system allows for the submission of amendments electronically and according to the Centre for Informatics the uptake was very positive. Fifty per cent of the amendments proposed were submitted electronically and some PGs submitted amendments only electronically.[34] This type of system allows for a more efficient management of the amendments submitted, as well as of the voting process, therefore enhancing the process of consideration of bills. It also makes the whole process more transparent.

The impact of ICT on internal parliamentary work has therefore been patchy. The Intranet has played an important role in making MPs (and staff) use the digital means of communication increasingly, just as Resolution 68/ 2003 has made PGs more compliant with the digital means of communication; but there is still a lot to do. ICTs have made work more efficient and transparent, but this needs to be more embedded in the practices of MPs and parliamentary staff in order to have a real impact. This is a time of real change though, in the way the AR is integrating the use of ICTs in parliamentary practice and a close eye should be kept on the forthcoming developments.

CONCLUSION

The AR is a relatively new parliament and one where a culture of secrecy has dominated up to the mid-1990s. Since then a slow process of change of culture and practices has made the AR a more open institution. ICTs have been a key part in this process.

ICTs have had an impact in facilitating parliamentary work by providing access to a much wider range of digital information, which MPs use and appreciate. ICTs have also made the AR better known as an institution, in particular through its website and the possibility of contacting MPs by email. In a system typically dominated by the party as the main unit of representation, the access to MPs' emails has brought an extra dimension to the relationship between parliament and citizens. It has introduced a new layer of representation in a very rigid system where parliamentary identity usually blendes in with party identity and where MPs have little visibility. This is an area where ICTs have made a clear difference. In everything else the mediation by PG is predominant – something to which ICTs have not made much difference: parliament's compartmentalisation by PG is reproduced in most of the ICT structure and use. One area where this is less patent is the Intranet, one of the main engines of change in the use of ICTs in the Portuguese parliament.

As yet, the impact of the introduction of ICTs has been limited in changing Portuguese parliamentary activity. Currently, the AR's embedding of ICTs is mainly at a stage of 'dissemination of information' with some indication that it is moving towards the 'digital communication' era. One expects 2007 and 2008 to be crucial years in a move towards embedding ICTs in parliamentary practice, as many new initiatives are currently taking place in this area. These could have a significant impact in practices, particularly as MPs are generally optimistic about the potential of these new means. Importantly also, the AR is currently undergoing a time of political stability. As seen in previous processes of reform, political stability is a key condition for processes of change to reach their aims.[35] Still, one should not disregard that the expansion of ICTs will also bring new challenges, which MPs may find difficult to address if the current level of staff support remains unchanged.

ACKNOWLEDGEMENT

A substantial part of this article is based on research supported financially by the Institute of Applied Ethics, University of Hull, for which the author is very grateful, in particular Xiudian Dai for his efforts in securing funding. Special thanks also to Rosa Vicente-Merino for her work in collating the data and for many stimulating discussions on the topic. The author is also very grateful for the participation of all interviewees who have contributed to this research and, in particular, for the contributions from the Portuguese parliament's Centre for Informatics, Centre of Information to Citizens and Public Relations and Coordinating Team of the Project of the Parliament for Young People.

NOTES

1. See, for instance, S. Coleman, J. Taylor, *et al.* (eds.), *Parliament in the Age of the Internet* (Oxford: Oxford University Press, 1999) and S. Coleman and B. Nathanson, *Learning to Live with the Internet – How European parliamentarians are adapting to the digital age*, EPRI, available at www.epri.org/epriknowledge/contents/Studies.php (13 Feb. 2007), 2005; J. Hoff, S. Coleman. *et al.* (eds.), *Information Polity – Special Issue on Use of ICT by Members of Parliament*, 9/1–2 (2004), and A. Trechsel, R. Kies, *et al.*, *Evaluation of The Use of New Technologies in Order to Facilitate Democracy in Europe*, European Parliament, STOA 116 EN 10-2003, 2003, available at http://edc.unige.ch/edcadmin/images/ STOA.pdf (13 Feb. 2007), and S. Ward and W. Lusoli, '"From Weird to Wired": MPs, the Internet and Representative Politics in the UK', *The Journal of Legislative Studies*, 11/1 (2005).
2. C. Leston-Bandeira, 'The Impact of the Internet on Parliaments: a Legislative Studies Framework', *Parliamentary Affairs*, 60/4 (2007), forthcoming.
3. See, G. Cardoso, C. Cunha, and S. Nascimento, 'Ministers of Parliament and Information and Communicaton Technologies as a Means of Horizontal and Vertical Communication in Western Europe', *Information Polity – special Issue on Use of ICT by Members of Parliament*, 9/1–2, 2004, pp. 29–40, and G. Cardoso, C. Cunha, and S. Nascimento, 'Bridging the e-Democracy Gap in Portugal', *Information, Communication and Society*, 9/4 (2006), pp. 452–72.
4. Review of WebPages includes parliament's main page, as well as of its Intranet and of each PG. Questionnaires were sent to all Portuguese MPs in April 2005, with a response rate of 20.4 per cent. This was followed by in-depth interviews in June 2005. We carried out interviews with ten people, including parliamentary officials (2), PG-based staff (1) and MPs (7). The MPs were selected to represent the different PGs, as well as varying degrees of competence in ICT. The representation by PGs was as follows: two MPs for each of the two larger PGs (PS and PSD) and one for each of the smaller PGs (CDS-PP, PCP and BE; the PEV was the only PG not included because they did not reply to our requests) – see note (8) for details on each party. The selection in terms of ICT competence was done through the answers to the questionnaires, based on a rate of use of ICT. Among the seven MPs interviewed, two were classified as ICT proficient, three as ICT competent and two as ICT beginner. This research was integrated in a comparative project, which also included the British, European and Swedish parliaments. This article uses some data from the survey questionnaires applied in those parliaments for comparative purposes (response rates, respectively, 6.9, 7.9 and 24.9 per cent).

We will refer, in particular, to the European and Swedish cases, because they share a similar method of election of MPs.

5. Interviews in June 2005.

6. C. Leston-Bandeira, From *Legislation to Legitimation* (London: Routledge, 2004) p. 48.

7. According to information provided by parliament's Centre for Informatics and Centre of Information to Citizens and Public Relations – interviews in June 2005 complemented by emails exchange in March 2007.

8. DAR, II-A, n.118/IX/1, 30 July 2003, p. 4704.

9. The four Portuguese main parties are the CDS-PP (*Centro Democrático e Social- Partido Popular*) Christian democrat, Catholic; the PCP (*Partido Comunista Português*), communist; the PS (*Partido Socialista*), socialist/social democrat; the PSD (*Partido Social Democrata*) right liberal. Besides these four main parties, the last few legislatures have also included two other small parliamentary groups: the BE (*Bloco de Esquerda*), left wing with predominantly urban support, and the PEV (*Partido Os Verdes*), greens. The PS and the PSD have been the two larger parties sharing between themselves around 70 per cent of the vote and alternating in government. The current legislature, elected in Feb. 2005, has the following composition: PS (121 MPs), PSD (75 MPs), CDS-PP (12), PCP (12), BE (8) and PEV (2) (data from www.parlamento.pt/deputados/resultadoseleitorais/index.html, accessed 17April 2007). The AR has a total of 230 MPs.

10. Parliamentary Group of PS, *Remodelacao do website to GPPS*, available at http://www.ps.parlamento.pt/?menu=ajuda, (accessed 09 March 2007).

11. Interview with parliamentary official, 20 June 2006.

12. See diagram illustrating this division in: Portuguese Parliament, 'Use of Information and Communication Technologies at the Assembly of the Republic', Eighth EPRI Conference, Prague, 2006, available at www.epri.org/epriknowledge/8th_EPRI_conference/Down-loads.php (accessed 14 June 2006).

13. Although each email address should follow a set pattern of Initialoffirstname.Surname@par-ty. parlamento.pt, this is not always the case and there are numerous variations of the first part of the address (such as Justinitials@ or Fullfirstname.Surname@).

14. J. Viegas d'Abreu, 'From Paper to Full Electronic Legislative Procedure in the Portuguese Parliament', Ninth EPRI Conference, Lisbon, 2007, available at http://www.epri.org/epri-knowledge/9th_EPRI_Conference/9th_EPRI_Conference_Presentations.php (accessed 18 April 2007).

15. Information complemented by email, March 2007.

16. See explanation in note (4).

17. The retrieval of information is by far the main way Portuguese MPs use the internet, with 80 per cent of them saying they do this on a regular basis. In contrast, only 44 per cent say they use the Internet regularly to communicate with constituents (in comparison with 71 per cent and 80 per cent, respectively, in the European and Swedish parliaments) and 50 per cent to communicate with their party (in comparison with 59 and 80 per cent, respectively, in the European and Swedish parliaments).

18. C. Leston-Bandeira, 'Parliament and Citizens in Portugal: Still Looking for Links', in P. Norton (ed.), *Parliaments and Citizens in Western Europe* (London: Frank Cass, 2002), pp. 128–52.

19. *paginaspessoais.parlamento.pt*, available at http://paginaspessoais.parlamento.pt/ (accessed 13 Feb. 2007).

20. Former Speakers keep a special status as MPs having access to better resources than ordinary MPs.

21. *Sistema de Blogs da Assembleia da República*, available at http://blogs.parlamento.pt/indice/ (accessed 17 April 2007).

22. BE, *Portal do GP do BE*, http://beparlamento.esquerda.net/; PS, *Grupo Parlamentar do PS*, www.ps.parlamento.pt/(all accessed 08 March 2007).

23. CDS-PP, CDS-PP, available at www.cds.pt/website/pagina23.php (accessed 02 May 2007); PCP, *Partido Comunista Português – Assembleia da República*, available at http://www.pcp.pt/index.php?option=com_content&task=section&id=3&Itemid =120; PEV, *Partido*

Ecologista Os Verdes, available at http://www.osverdes.pt/index01.html; PSD, PSD – *Portal Social Democrata*, available at http://www.psd.pt/(accessed 8 March 2007).

24. *PS – Partido Socialista Braga*, available at http://www.psbraga.net (accessed 14 March 2007).
25. Interview in June 2005 complemented by email exchange in March 2007.
26. *Ligações*, available at www.parlamento.pt/ligacoes/index.html (accessed 8 March 2007).
27. *ARtv – Canal Parlamento*, available at www.canal.parlamento.pt (accessed 9 March 2007).
28. *Fórum – Espaço de Discussão*, available at www.parlamento.pt/forum pub (accessed 17 April 2007).
29. *O Direito de Petição*, available at www.parlamento.pt/peticoes/index.html (accessed 17 April 2007).
30. Information provided by the Centre of Information to Citizens and Public Relations in email exchange, March 2007.
31. Information provided by the Coordinating Team of the Project of the Parliament for Young People in emails exchange, March 2007.
32. Contrary to the conclusions reached in G. Cardoso, C. Cunha and S. Nascimento, 'Bridging the e-Democracy Gap in Portugal', based on earlier research, indicating therefore some change in this area.
33. Special mention could also be made of the Committee on European Affairs; the only committee with a website.
34. Information provided through email exchange, March 2007.
35. C. Leston-Bandeira, 'The Portuguese Parliament and Public Opinion: A Case for Reform?', *The Journal of Legislative Studies*, 8/2 (2002).

Becoming Electronic Parliamentarians? ICT Usage in the Swedish Riksdag

MAGNUS LINDH and LEE MILES

The inclusion of the Swedish Parliament (Riksdag) in any comparative study of the role of media technologies on parliamentary behaviour is logical.[1] In general, Sweden as a country maintains a reputation for being one of the leaders in Europe in terms of ICT usage by its population (in per capita terms) and the political and economic elites.[2] The expectation of many would be that the Riksdag should be one of the best legislative laboratories, where high levels of ICT usage among parliamentarians could be discovered and should represent the 'top end' in terms of the comparison with the legislatures of Britain, Portugal and the European Union (EU). It may be that it is in Sweden where we may see, at first hand, how concepts of an evolving, if sometimes fuzzy, 'Electronic Democracy' (ED) work out alongside, and react with, more deep-seated conventions of open and transparent democratic practice.[3]

So far, as mentioned by Cristina Leston-Bandeira in her article, most scholars of legislative studies have been interested in how *individual* parliamentarians have adapted to (the potential of) ICT, and the extent to which parliamentarians use such technology in providing services, like information on their websites and the degree of utilisation of email when communicating with constituents. In essence, to discover the 'state of play' and the level of parliamentary activity, largely by MPs, undertaken through, or affected by, ICT usage.

Previous studies of Swedish parliamentarians and ICT usage have been no different.[4] As Zittel comments, there has been 'little interest to link new forms of digital participation at the individual level with actual political structures and to define specific policies of institutional reform'.[5] Hence, there has been divergence among political scientists about how existing political structures (taken here to mean political party organisations and institutional authorities in the legislature) react to greater ICT usage among parliamentarians. The intention of this study is not to go over old ground, apart from providing a brief update on ICT usage among Swedish parliamentarians, but rather to initiate discussion on the implications for party organisations and legislative institutions that have been the central platform for individual MPs in the past.

THE ORGANISATIONAL AND INSTITUTIONAL CONTEXT

It is important to outline conceptual distinctions that will underpin the analyses undertaken later. In broad terms, we recognise the significance of three particular dimensions relating to ICT usage. First, there is the *individual dimension* – namely MPs developing and utilising personal ICT services, such as personal websites and political blogs – provided independently of party or parliamentary facilities. Second, there is the *organisational dimensions* – these are the ICT services provided by the political party organisations, such as, the Swedish Social Democratic Party (SAP) – that provide ICT facilities and party-based websites for their respective parliamentary MPs and thus operate under a collective identity with overtly partisan objectives. Third, there is the (legislative) *institutional dimension* – namely the role of the parliamentary institution (in this case the Riksdag) – in providing broad ICT functions and a website for the entire legislature, as well as (sometimes) guidelines on management of their usage and conduct with an emphasis on ensuring that all facilities are offered on a non-partisan basis.

Greater ICT usage among individual MPs may have, in the context of this study, important implications for both party organisations (organisational dimension) and/or the legislative institutions (institutional dimension). First, new ICT forums, such as political blogs, might facilitate spontaneous virtual dialogue that is hard for organisations and institutions to manage. Second, greater individual ICT usage may lead to some internal restructuring and a reduction in hierarchies, since individual MPs may be 'empowered electronically' even in a political system such as Sweden, where there are strong

MP loyalties to their respective political parties. They may be less reliant upon the former for information and, potentially, may be less deferential to party or institutional leaderships. Third, greater ICT usage might accelerate organisational pluralism. The Internet may provide individual MPs with greater opportunities to establish new political networks outside the party or parliamentary sphere; although as Vedel argues, ED may over-hype the benefits of ICTs partly because it assumes, in its various forms, a demanding conception of citizenship and their participatory behaviour, an intricate notion of political transparency, a view of democracy that is reduced merely to aspects of debate and forecasts the demise of intermediary bodies, such as party organisations.[6]

As already discussed in this volume, an important question for political scholars, when moving beyond the level of the individual MPs to examine issues affecting party organisations and parliamentary institutions, is to what extent these party organisations and/or parliamentary institutions will respond either passively or actively to the challenges of ICTs. On the one hand, political party organisations may not pay much attention on the whole. They will be largely reactive and respond only if and when their MPs develop new forms of contact outside the traditional party organisations. Similarly, at the institutional level, the legislatures and their governing authorities will be passive actors content on facilitating, from an institutional viewpoint, the activity of parliamentarians.

On the other hand, party organisations and the institutional legislative authorities will (want to) ensure that the conduct of their associated parliamentarians will not have negative repercussions for them in the future.[7] In some instances, computer networks may reinforce the established political organisations rather than transforming them[8] with party organisations and, to a lesser extent, parliamentary authorities, using 'their pre-existing power resources and advantages to control and neutralise any pluralist tendencies of the new media'.[9]

ICTs, and especially websites, provide parties with new marketing devices to attract members, while the Internet may offer ways for party organisations to stimulate greater political participation since e-voting, e-polling, e-consultation and e-petitions provide further additions to 'the arsenals of political organisations and activists'[10], even if many of these instruments mainly replicate offline practices.[11] For many, the existence of established political parties, if coherent and well-organised, is critical since they would seek to sustain their long standing role as the intermediaries between citizens and MPs by offering ICT services to their respective parliamentarians that will, directly or indirectly, allow them to exercise some control over parliamentary behaviour and help to protect their strategic position between the parliamentarian and the voter.[12]

For parliamentary institutions, there is the potential to transmit vast quantities of information on parliamentary rationales, conduct and ongoing business.[13] It is important for parliamentary institutions to sustain public trust if they are to survive in their current forms or, alternatively, to allow their constituent members to push for institutional or constitutional reform, believing that ICTs could 'increase the administrative efficiency of the institution, improve information access and dissemination, and finally enhance MPs' and assemblies' interaction with citizens'.[14]

This article has two main objectives. First, we update the findings of previous studies of the Riksdag on ICT usage among Swedish parliamentarians. A survey of Swedish parliamentarians was carried out by Zittel and his conclusions, based on 2000 data, are reviewed against our evaluation carried out in 2005–06. Second, we analyse the responses of, and management by, party organisations and parliamentary institutions in relation to the ICT behaviour of individual MPs.

ICT USAGE IN THE SWEDISH RIKSDAG

In general terms, the party list system used for Swedish general elections has implications since, according to Zittel, MPs were cautious in making individual choices in networked communication.[15] Zittel suggested, for example, that there was some evidence that those Swedish MPs reliant on personal votes had a higher propensity to have a website, but this was also not statistically important and thus, there was no electoral connection with MPs choices of networked communication. Whatever the case, Swedish MPs operate in a parliamentary environment where there is a tendency for party organisations (organisational dimension) and legislative authorities (institutional dimension), rather than individual members, to take the lead. Swedish members share a parliamentary culture where the expectation is normally that the party organisation and institution-based actors provide services to MPs, ICTs or otherwise.[16] Yet, the results for ICT usage in 2000, indicated a (then) poor level of individualised digital communication in parliament, and this, according to Zittel, may have reflected the weak institutional position of MPs more broadly; given that individual Swedish parliamentarians had limited budgets and staff at their disposal. In effect, there were environmental, and possibly institutional, constraints that influenced MPs and their choice of websites.[17]

The results of our 2005 surveys of websites and 87 specific Swedish parliamentarians shed light on the extent of ICT usage among MPs and the forms of parliamentary political communication. The observation that ICT usage and its impact on Swedish political life have grown is reflected in, and verified by, our more contemporary evaluations. Three techniques are used in order to create a picture of Swedish e-Democracy. The first is a (primarily quantitative) survey of the use of personal websites by parliamentarians, conducted in 2005. The second is to evaluate, using quantitative evaluation and qualitative interviews (the latter undertaken in 2005–06), the extent to which Swedish parliamentarians use the Internet as a working tool. Finally, the degree of interactivity that parliamentarians are trying to achieve with citizens is evaluated. Assessments of the degree of interactivity rely primarily on more qualitative techniques and data, such as interviews with parliamentarians and staff in the Riksdag.

Turning to the first aspect, our 2005 survey indicates a substantial evolution from the position presented in the study by Zittel that used data from 2000. In Zittel's study, published in 2003, more than 70 per cent of the Swedish parliamentarians claimed that they did not have a website.[18] Digital communication was, at that point, not decentralised in the Riksdag, since parliamentary committees were not using websites and, for the most part, only a minority of members were on the web in 2000. Even senior parliamentarians displayed limited enthusiasm for ICT usage since the party leaderships did not have a presence on the web.[19] In our 2005 study, over 80 per cent of the parliamentarians answered that they now maintain a personal website (see Table 1). All Swedish MPs in the Riksdag, in 2005, also publicised an individual, official email address in their websites and the survey results show that 89 per cent of those websites surveyed incorporated clear references to MPs' individual contact details. There are indications that Swedish parliamentarians are providing the minimal electronic services that the vast majority of citizens want – namely a website presence and a clear and accessible email address.[20]

This result is interesting in several ways. First, there has been a dramatic increase in how many individual parliamentarians have entered the realms of cyberspace, as indicated by the rising numbers of personal websites. This was also confirmed in the qualitative interviews. Not a single interviewee believed

TABLE 1
DO YOU HAVE A PERSONAL WEBSITE?

	No. of Respondents	Percentage	Valid Percentage	Cumulative Percentage
Valid				
Yes	70	80.5	81.4	81.4
No	16	18.4	18.6	100.0
Total	86	98.9	100.0	
Missing				
999	1	1.1		
Total	87	100.0		

that it would be possible in the future to be a successful politician without maintaining a personal website. Nevertheless, there were differences among respondents as to their degree of personal involvement in the maintenance of their personal websites – activity was, in some cases, devolved to support staff. Yet, the quantitative survey also shows a higher propensity to maintain personal websites, as well as stronger value placed on them by Swedish MPs.

Second, however, there is uncertainty over the relationship between personal websites and staff pages provided on the organisational websites of the political parties. Further research needs to be undertaken on definitions of personal websites since there has been an increase not just in the number of personal websites provided by MPs, but also in the ambitions of the party organisations in offering staff-pages on individual members, on their corporate websites. Such differences raise ethical issues of control for individual MPs regarding the content and format of their respective individual details on corporate websites and who, ultimately, is responsible and accountable for the content.

When the 2005 results are tabulated in terms of gender, party affiliation and age of responding MPs, there are also deviations from those discovered by Zittel. As regards gender comparison, there seems to be some statistical difference between the sexes (see Table 2). If anything, proportionally more male have personal websites than female MPs, although it would be hard to argue that this implies a greater interest in ICT usage among male rather than female MPs *per se*. However, there are more discernible patterns, when it comes to party affiliation and age.

As regards whether there are any differences in ICT usage according to party affiliation, then an ideological 'left–right' dimension can be detected. Over 80 per cent of those MPs registering 'no' answers, and thus not having

TABLE 2
GENDER AND THE EXISTENCE OF A PERSONAL WEBSITE?

		Do you have a personal website?		
		Yes	No	Total
Gender				
Female	Count	28	7	35
	Percentage within 'Do you have a personal website?'	40.0	43.8	40.7
Male	Count	42	9	51
	Percentage within 'Do you have a personal website?'	60.0	56.3	59.3
Total	Count	70	16	86
	Percentage within 'Do you have a personal website?'	100.0	100.0	100.0

personal websites, came from the Left Party and the social democrats – representing the mainstay of the 'socialist bloc' in the Riksdag. None of the eight Left Party representatives participating in our survey (out of a total number of 28) have a personal website (see Table 3) and the interviews with their respective party officials and MPs also suggest a reluctance to develop personal websites. Nevertheless, one cannot infer that our findings imply that no Left Party parliamentarians have personal websites or that they are resistant to ongoing ICT innovation. A brief assessment of the Left Party's organisational website shows that one MP has a personal website[21] and six of their 28 parliamentarians have a political blog (see later).

Interestingly, Zittel argued that if website presence is correlated against the ages and electoral districts of parliamentarians, then younger MPs have higher propensity to utilise personal websites, but there is no real significant relationship found between the size, type or geographical location of electoral districts and networked communication. As regards the age factor, he, therefore, suggested that it requires generational change in parliamentarians before ICT usage becomes highly significant and that a discernible increased use of networked communication could be detected.[22]

Nonetheless, our results indicate that such assertions may need qualification. The 2005 survey shows that there is a majority without personal websites

TABLE 3
PARTY AND THE EXISTENCE OF A PERSONAL WEBSITE?

| | | Do you have a personal website? | | |
		Yes	No	Total
Party				
Social democratic	Count	20	5	25
	percentage within 'Do you have a personal website?'	28.6	31.3	29.1
Moderate	Count	13	1	14
	percentage within 'Do you have a personal website?'	18.6	6.3	16.3
Liberal	Count	17	0	17
	percentage within 'Do you have a personal website?'	24.3	0.0	19.8
Christian dem	Count	6	0	6
	percentage within 'Do you have a personal website?'	8.6	0.0	7.0
Left	Count	0	8	8
	percentage within 'Do you have a personal website?'	0.0	50.0	9.3
Centre	Count	8	2	10
	percentage within 'Do you have a personal website?'	11.4	12.5	11.6
Green	Count	6	0	6
	percentage within 'Do you have a personal website?'	8.6	0.0	7.0
Total	Count	70	16	86
	percentage within 'Do you have a personal website?'	100.0	100.0	100.0

among MPs aged between 46 and 60, which may confirm that the take-up rate among older generations of parliamentarians is slower than among younger MPs. However, the responses for elder MPs is also important since all respective parliamentarians over the age of 61 indicated that they maintained a personal website (see Table 4). This was also confirmed by the respective qualitative interviews with older parliamentarians. It was suggested that they, in a personal capacity, did not believe that a generational factor existed in practice, since many older legislators and their offices were actively using ICTs in their political life.

The 2005 survey also raises an interesting conceptual question in terms of the individual dynamics, affecting Swedish MPs. Given the growing numbers of personal websites, further work needs to be carried out on two issues. First, on the practical relationship and linkages between personal websites and those individual staff pages offered on broader party organisational websites. Second, whether a qualitative distinction between types of Swedish parliamentarians in terms of their ICT usage should be made – between those who are *ICT reactionists* and are, more or less, simply responding to what are considered the new acceptable norms of parliamentary communication and those that are *ICT activists* who are enthusiastically seeking to push the boundaries and offer new avenues of communication between legislators and citizens and parliamentarians and their party organisations. A good example of such ICT activists would be Moderate Party MP, Tobias Billström. He argued that his website now represented 'his political heart' with the parliament acting more as a complement. According to him, his website is his point of departure when he acts as a politician. Although this may be too

TABLE 4
AGE AND THE EXISTENCE OF A PERSONAL WEBSITE?

		Do you have a personal website?		
		Yes	No	Total
Age				
Under 30	Count	3	0	3
	percentage within 'Do you have a personal website?'	4.3	0.0	3.5
31 to 45	Count	18	4	22
	percentage within 'Do you have a personal website?'	25.7	25.0	25.6
46 to 60	Count	37	12	49
	percentage within 'Do you have a personal website?'	52.9	75.0	57.0
61 and over	Count	12	0	12
	percentage within 'Do you have a personal website?'	17.1	0.0	14.0
Total	Count	70	16	86
	percentage within 'Do you have a personal website?'	100.0	100.0	100.0

ambitious for the majority of Swedish, largely ICT reactive parliamentarians, there is much to suggest that, at least in the Swedish case, the debate will continue on how the use of ICTs and e-Democracy can strengthen concepts of parliamentary accessibility and transparency.[23]

This more contemporary evaluation also challenges Zittel's assumptions about the impact of electoral influences on ICT usage. Interviews undertaken in 2005–06 suggest that Swedish MPs are aware of the growing electoral pressures, especially given the proximity of the 2006 General Election. The qualitative interviews suggest that a small number of MPs have gone outside these normal channels. Some MPs, such as Tobias Billström, have taken up services offered by outside private IT firms, and interestingly the country's tax system permits deductions to be made for these types of costs if paid from the MP's own pockets. Nevertheless, the overall impression from the interviews was that, at least at the institutional level, the Riksdag provides extensive ICT services, with opportunities for training and support being offered to MPs by the ICT personnel.

As a second indicator, the survey question: 'To what extent do you use the Internet as a work tool?' was asked. There were three possible answers: do not use it, 0–2 hours per day and more than 2 hours per day. The results show that over 60 per cent of parliamentarians use the Internet for more than 2 hours per day (see Table 5). As a proportion of the work-related activities of parliamentarians, more than 2 hours can be regarded as a high figure.

ICT activity is also a reflection of a growing confidence among Swedish parliamentarians that, according to the interviewees, ICTs are well integrated into parliamentary work. It may also reflect a growing interconnection between the individual and the organisational and institutional dimensions. At the institutional level, the Riksdag meets the ICT needs of most parliamentarians, such as, laptops and advanced mobile phones, with hardware usually replaced every third year. Growing ICT usage could then simply reflect the

TABLE 5
THE EXTENT OF USAGE OF THE INTERNET BY THE PARLIAMENTARIAN AS A
WORK TOOL?

	No. of Respondents	Percentage	Valid Percentage	Cumulative Percentage
Valid				
0–2 hours per day	32	36.8	37.6	37.6
More than 2 hours per day	53	60.9	62.4	100.0
Total	85	97.7	100.0	
Missing 999	2	2.3		
Total	87	100.0		

better ICT provision by the Riksdag in 2005 that has increased the attractiveness of ICTs for MPs.

Political communication *via* ICTs between parliamentarians and their party organisations has also extensively increased and become normal practice, even though the MPs interviewed consistently claimed that there is a problem of finding the time to deal with accelerating e-communication and raised fears that qualitative political dialogue is in danger. As one parliamentarian puts it: 'If we've got more and more then I think we need of course a control on it because it's impossible to have the time, and email can't replace talking (sic)'.[24]

Greater ICT usage can also be attributed to the growing acknowledgement among MPs that key groups of citizens are simply more ICT-savvy. Liberal Party MP, Crister Winbäck, for example, argued that this was linked to generational change, 'because when the younger people in Sweden are going to be interested in politics they will use, of course, ICT tools, as they are doing already. We are trying to see the statistics for the website and we are seeing that it's increasing'.[25] Hence, greater usage of the Internet as a parliamentary work tool reflects organisational dynamics, institutional inducement and the broader demands of citizens as perceived by legislators in the Riksdag.

As a third indicator, Zittel showed that the degree of interaction on the Swedish parliamentarian's websites were very low in 2000 and that parliamentarians had very limited ambitions in terms of utilising the potential of websites, since the interactivity of the websites in the Riksdag was minimal. In 2000 at least, few Swedish members used websites to increase public dialogue in practice with only very limited inclusion of discussion boards, hardly any online surveys featuring in the design of websites and only very limited textual information being carried.[26] In other works, this low level of interactivity and limited content matter on MPs' websites suggested that Swedish parliamentarians were not using websites to convey information on parliamentary process. Above all, where individual websites were apparent, their content largely failed to differ much from that already provided by more traditional hard copy forms of information. ICTs were in effect, adding little in practice to Swedish practices of openness and transparency.

Our quantitative survey (2005) and qualitative interviews (2005–06) present a mixed picture of development since 2000. It was found that, in general, there was an improving, if still rather low, scale of interactivity on the websites of Swedish parliamentarians. Under five per cent of the 255 Swedish websites examined were categorised as having 'high' or 'very high' levels of interactivity, with nearly 80 per cent of them being placed in the 'very low' category (see Table 6). Only nine per cent of them incorporated e-bulletin facilities, barely three per cent of them included guest book or question and answer sections and only 2.4 per cent of them encompassed

TABLE 6
SCALE OF INTERACTIVITY OF THE WEBSITES OF SWEDISH PARLIAMENTARIANS

	No. of Websites	Percentage	Valid Percentage	Cumulative Percentage
Valid				
Missing	22	8.6	8.6	8.6
Very low	203	79.6	79.6	88.2
Low	18	7.1	7.1	95.3
High	4	1.6	1.6	96.9
Very high	8	3.1	3.1	100.0
Total	255	100.0	100.0	

message-board or forum facilities. Most existing websites still inform rather than engage citizens.[27]

Nevertheless, the qualitative interviews suggest that Swedish parliamentarians are increasingly recognising that 'the interactive elements of new technologies provide significant opportunities to create far more channels through which to engage in the political process'.[28] Since party websites tend to include information that will be accessed primarily by the politically active sympathisers and supporters, MPs are interested in the potential for email, political blogs and online discussion and consultations that may help to broaden dialogue with citizens.[29] As one of our interviewees put it, MPs are interested 'in any means to get their message out'.[30]

In all the interviews, MPs were keen to show that they have considered how to make their websites attractive and more interactive. All of the respondents have considered creating a 'political blog' (if they did not already have one).[31] In particular, the majority of interviewed parliamentarians recognised that a blog has the potential to facilitate a high degree of interactivity with the constituents. By 2005, the ICT picture has, in qualitative terms at least, moved on from that of 2000. On the Social Democratic Party's website (the organisational dimension), for instance, there are web-links to nearly 200 blogs run by, or associated with, party representatives. More specifically, 15 of these blogs are run by individual SAP MPs. On the Moderate Party (Conservatives) website, for example, there are 60 links to political blogs, of which five were being run by MPs.[32] The political blog may be one of the most significant new features influencing Swedish political life, at least from 2005.[33]

A relevant question is whether a political blog represents merely a contemporary trend in ICT usage or whether it will evolve into a more permanent feature of Swedish parliamentary practice. In the Swedish context at least, this will be difficult to conclude for some time, since the rise in the number of political blogs may reflect the fact that MPs are developing their online profiles to aid in campaigning before and during the 2006 General Election. Yet, the existence of increasing numbers of political blogs may suggest a common desire among Swedish MPs of all political persuasions to carve out an online presence that is cheaper and more prolific than the websites and thus offer direct and indirect campaigning opportunities at a key time in the electoral cycle.

The value of political blogs in fostering a closer relationship with voters is also a moot point. Although the interviewees recognised that blogs offered the chance for MPs to present their views in a personal manner, there still remains some ambiguity as to their level of involvement in the actual running of their political blogs. Given the demands on their time, many MPs delegated their management to subordinates and thus the degree of individual members' input varies considerably across the existing political blogs . Yet, the potential of political blogs for Swedish parliamentarians is substantial. Since political blogs can attract interaction with citizens who may not actually be from the MP's respective constituency and thus may not be the direct voters for the individual MP, it should not be forgotten either that MPs are also, in most cases, career politicians anxious to make a broader impact on political discourses and debates. Blogging, for instance, may offer additional and alternative attractions not for parliamentarians in their role as constituency MPs, but rather as a political tool for advancing MPs' profiles among citizens *per se* and thereby perhaps contributing to career advancement.

Nevertheless, the interviews also indicate a degree of uncertainty among parliamentarians about *how* to use the political blog as a tool to further their political career; with interviewees being cautious about how to differentiate between each political blog so as to identify those that are the more influential and/or have the largest dissemination in this expanding 'blogosphere'. Given that, for example, the Social Democratic Party website (organisational dimension) includes nearly 200 links to political blogs, where party members discus issues, the message of individual MPs may become confused or marginalised, The media analyst Alexander Mason argues, for instance, that the most important political effect of a blog depends ultimately on if and when the traditional media catch on to it, and highlight the content featured in the blog.[34] Hence, a primary consideration for MPs when considering the political value of blogging, and whether indeed to run one, remains on how to ensure that such a personal blog can attract the attention of the media to look at it.[35]

THE CHALLENGES FOR PARTY ORGANISATIONS AND PARLIAMENTARY INSTITUTIONS

As shown in the previous section, Swedish MPs are becoming electronic parliamentarians; there has been a gradual expansion in ICT usage by them, not only in terms of providing key services such as email addresses and personal websites, but also in a growing appreciation among Riksdag members of the potential opportunities offered by even newer forms of interactivity, such as political blogging. There is some evidence of greater individualisation, whereby parliamentarians have the potential to develop more direct and intense forms of political dialogue with citizens. Rather ironically, citizens may be increasingly aware that these more interactive ICTs, for example political blogs, can extend the relationship with their MP in new directions and thus they may want their parliamentarians 'to do more, but not necessarily more of the same'.[36] This creates further pressures on the party organisations and parliamentary institution since any such unaddressed deficiencies may have indirect consequences for these broader collective entities in terms of voter support (for party organisations) and citizen loyalty and trust (for the legislative institution), and thus may prompt them to 'rethink their new (and old) media engagement strategies'.[37]

In the Swedish case, there is much to suggest that parliamentarians prefer it, if traditional party organisations and legislative institutional authorities were to take the lead with this. As Esaiasson and Holmberg have concluded in the past, the Swedish representative system is characterised as being 'run from above' with elite structures, such as strong and disciplined political parties, providing a natural comfort zone for the activities of most Swedish parliamentarians.[38] If Sweden remains 'a party controlled system',[39] it is highly likely that the organisations that 'run from above' will be best placed to accommodate the new ICT challenges deriving from greater 'interactivity from below', for Riksdag members.

Although there may be common challenges for party organisations and legislative institutions, it is likely that the strategies they follow may differ in terms of ambition and content. Part of this derives from the fact that party organisations and parliamentary institutions operate in a slightly different context with diverging mission statements. The relationship between the individual member and their party organisation is qualitatively different from that between the individual member and the parliamentary institution in which they reside.

The relationship between individual MP and party organisation is a strong one and the party organisation may want to maximise the management and control over the format, integrity and content of MP websites in order to enhance the potential to present a good (and common) image to voters. With some simplification, party organisations and MPs share a common objective – 'they want to place partisan material on their site telling the public how good they and their party are and how rotten the other side is'.[40] Party organisations, at least when it comes to ICTs, may want to be active and involved in order to engage citizens and voters. Although used sparsely by parliamentarians at the moment, recent innovations, for example e-newsletters on their personal websites, can fulfil an overtly partisan role – namely in promoting party policy.[41]

The 2005–06 interviews suggest that parliamentarians are clearly under the impression that the party organisations want to take control, even if this has not always happened on a practical level. A key question is, to what extent party organisations can accommodate the heterogeneity of, and be accountable for, the ICT behaviour of their respective MPs. Recent Swedish political episodes suggest that party organisations are waking up to this issue.

In autumn 2005, for instance, there was an ICT conducted political scandal relating to the leader of the Moderate Party, Fredrik Reinfeldt, who was allegedly the victim of a concerted email campaign of slander among certain political commentators. On 23 February 2006, this campaign was exposed and the sender of the email was traced to the headquarters of the Social Democratic Party. The Party's organisational response was very quick. The Party Secretary, Marita Ulvskog, interrupted her holiday to deal with this scandal and only two days later, the party leadership claimed that they had found 'the individual responsible for the slander' who consequently resigned from his post. The party organisation's strategy was to move the attention, and responsibility, away from the Party (organisational dimension) to the individual (individual dimension). As a consequence, there was a short debate in the Swedish media focusing on the ethical questions connected to ICT usage and notions of party and individual accountability. The right wing (*borgerliga alliansen*) parties invited other parties to enter discussion across the political spectrum on the relationship between political ethics and accountability and ICTs. In response, the Social Democrats argued that this discussion is already ongoing, and introduced internally an IT-policy for ethical issues and the upcoming election.[42]

This was followed, some three months later, by another ICT-disseminated scandal involving the Prime Minister's closest advisor, State Secretary Lars Danielsson. Two representatives of the Liberal Party (*Folkpartiet*) mentioned rumours of Danielsson having a mistress in their political blogs, and SAP politicians argued that the Liberals had fallen into the same ICT-related trap as they had done a few months earlier. The response from the Liberal Party leadership differed from that of the SAP in the earlier case. Liberal Party leader, Lars Leijonborg, expressed regret in public about the events, but took no action at the party level (organisational dimension), arguing that he could not possibly control what thousands of individual liberals write about in political blogs.[43]

For party organisations, blogging may have been an important tool in the party campaigns for the 2006 General Election, representing a kind of battle for power over the 'blogosphere'. Certainly, the respective party organisations were increasingly conscious that this was the case. The Social Democrats, for instance, hired the American expert, Joe Trippi, a former advisor to the American Democrat presidential candidate, Howard Dean, in recognition that Dean's ICT-savvy campaign had been successful in maximising the potential of the Internet for party campaigning. Stig-Björn Ljunggren predicted that there would be two parallel election campaign strategies used in the 2006 General Election; one emanating from the headquarters, and a more politically dubious and 'dirty' variant conducted by the grassroots in the 'blogosphere'.

Whether this was entirely the case is unclear. Yet, the party organisations did have to respond to unpredictable, and potentially politically risky challenges associated with Internet usage and political blogging, during the 2006 election campaigns. On 3 September 2006, for instance, a major political scandal erupted when the SAP accused Liberal Party activists of gaining access to the SAP-intranet (SAPnet) by using login codes from a local SAP office, and the episode remains the subject of a police investigation. Again the Liberal Party leader, Lars Leijonborg was, at this point, able to escape embroilment in scandal, although it resulted in the party organisation appointing an Ethical Committee (*etikkomission*) to explore the ethical implications of such ICT-related activity.[44]

In contrast, in the institutional context, the functions of parliamentary authorities are often determinedly non-partisan; it is seen as essential that institutional authorities are not perceived as supporting explicit partisan political activities, and thus members are restricted in drawing upon the public resources of the Riksdag to enhance their prospects. The implication is that this constrains the deployment and use of ICTs by the Riksdag to support MPs. Moreover, the role of parliamentary institutional bodies is more to provide electronic tools and facilities to aid the work of MPs and this may simply not be the same as actually empowering the members. As Ward and Vedel have highlighted, the participatory context is clearly influential since this may help determine – 'who controls the agenda for electronic discussion? What are the rules of access? How do the existing rules of an organisation incorporate electronic channels? And is participation viewed as important?'[45]

According to the interviews, the parliamentarians suggest that the Riksdag's authorities (institutional dimension) provide a high level of ICT support and express equally high levels of satisfaction with existing ICT provision. Indeed, the level of financial support provided by the institution to parliamentarians has increased substantially following the 2006 General Election, from an amount that covers salary costs for a ratio of 1 assistant per five MPs, to an improved ration of one assistant to one MP. Nevertheless, since this financial support is also distributed through party allocations, there remains some tension among the party organisations and the legislative authorities about to what extent, partisan and non-partisan rationales, may become blurred.

Given that MPs derive their authority from their voters, this also constrains the ability of parliament to act as a corporate body for its members on how they should carry out their duties.[46] The Riksdag has restricted its attention to rules on issues of propriety, such as the financing of MPs activities, yet there remain very few institutional constraints (so far) on their behaviour when using new media technologies. In many ways, parliamentary authorities may be more involved in informing citizens and voters.

However, our research also highlights tensions affecting the institutional context (institutional dimension) since there are clearly internal divisions within parliamentary authorities on their role in providing ICT facilities. In the Riksdag, for instance, the Department of Information has extended ICT usage as much as possible among MPs, while the different Standing Committees have developed their own conventions that are not always compatible with e-democracy. At the same time, the IT department appears reluctant to replace existing (and always the most functional from an ICT perspective) systems. There is a tension between the political opportunities of ICT usage and the practical delivery of ICT facilities.

Interviews with members of the Riksdag's IT department suggest that there are four main issues for non-partisan legislative authorities: hardware – software compatibility issues; the need to establish institutional wide procedures for ICT usage among Standing Committees in order to maximise the potential of ICTs; compatibility between the ICT facilities of parliament and the executive to aid MPs access to government documents and improve accountability and the storage of digital archives in the future.[47] These are the practical ICT issues that affect the principle of Swedish openness and transparency. The Riksdag identified the potential for ICTs to maximise openness and transparency rather early and introduced guidelines and strategies in 2000 and 2001.[48] This should be compared with the comparatively slow response of the party organisations to introduce comparable guidelines on ICT behaviour and norms, with, for example, the SAP and the Liberals starting to discuss a party policy only in 2006 in response to the various recent political scandals.

In our view, it will be the party organisations rather than the parliament's institutional bodies that will be more influential and dominant in shaping the e-agenda and the preferences of individual MPs on ICT issues. After all, the Swedish system has a robust party system where MPs allegiances to party structures remain strong, and it is the party organisations that have a more assertive interest; an overtly partisan motive that will engage the minds of MPs and the power and resources to provide common platforms, guidelines, facilities and expertise to enable individual MPs to get the best out of future ICT usage.

Regarding future research, we suggest that, first, there is a need to explore the tensions within and between the individual, organisational and institutional dimensions of ICT usage. Secondly, in order to understand organisational influences and responses to ICTs, greater attention needs to be placed on defining personal websites and their relationship to staff pages on the party organisations' websites. Do they operate for different arenas and with different logics? Are there compatibility and management control issues at play, given that MPs appear on a party website as part of a political organisational entity, but also include links from such sites to a more personally profiled website? Thirdly, investigations need to be broadened so that the expansion of blogging, rather than websites, is a central feature of any future evaluation. In July 2006, the party websites of the two largest Swedish political parties contained nearly 260 links to political blogs, including some 20 links to blogs of parliamentarians; while the recent scandals connected with political blogging in Sweden before and during the 2006 General Election campaigns may indicate that blogging is a main feature of ICT advanced political systems. It is important to ascertain if and how parliamentarians use blogs to attract the attention of the media in order to get their political views and profile across to citizens. Looking to the future, there may be further attempts by party organisations and the Riksdag to try to establish codes of conduct in order to clarify organisational and institutional accountability for the content of political blogs.

NOTES

1. This article is based on a paper delivered at the Seventh Workshop of Parliamentary Scholars and Parliamentarians, Wroxton College, Oxfordshire, (29 July 2006) and the second Karlstad Seminar on Studying Political Action, Swedish Political Studies Association conference, Karlstad University, Sweden (12 October 2006).
2. For example, see J. Åström, 'Digital Voting, Ideas, Intentions and Initiatives in Swedish Local Governments', in R. Gibson, A. Römmele and S. Ward (eds.), *Electronic Democracy: Mobilisation, Organisation and Participation via New ICTs*, (London: Routledge, 2004).
3. T. Zittel, 'Electronic Democracy and Electronic Parliaments: A Comparison between the US House, the Swedish Riksdagen and the German Bundestag', paper presented to the Joint Sessions of Workshops of the European Consortium of Political Research, Grenoble, 6–11 April 2001.
4. See T. Zittel, 'Political Representation in the Networked Society: The Americanisation of European Systems of Responsible Party Government', *Journal of Legislative Studies*, 9/3 (2003), pp. 32–53.
5. See Zittel, 'Electronic Democracy and Electronic Parliaments: A Comparison between the US House, the Swedish Riksdagen and the German Bundestag', p. 6.
6. T. Vedel, 'The Idea of Electronic Democracy: Origins, Visions and Questions', *Parliamentary Affairs*, 59/2 (2006), pp. 232–4.
7. Vedel, 'The Idea of Electronic Democracy: Origins, Visions and Questions', p. 230.

8. See S. Coleman, J. Taylor and W. van de Donk (eds.) *Parliament in the Age of the Internet*, (Oxford: Oxford University Press, 1999).
9. S.Ward and T. Vedel, 'Introduction: The Potential of the Internet Revisited', *Parliamentary Affairs*, 59/2 (2006), p. 210.
10. See S. Ward, R. Gibson and W. Lusoli, 'Online Participation and Mobilisation in Britain: Hype, Hope and Reality', *Parliamentary Affairs*, 56/4 (2003), p. 655.
11. S. Coleman and J. Spiller, 'Exploring New Media Effects in Representative Democracy', *Journal of Legislative Studies*, 9/3 (2003), p. 11.
12. See Zittel, 'Political Representation in the Networked Society: The Americanisation of European Systems of Responsible Party Government', p. 34.
13. See Ward, Gibson and Lusoli, 'Online Participation and Mobilisation in Britain: Hype, Hope and Reality', pp. 653–4.
14. W. Lusoli, S. Ward and R.Gibson, '(Re)connecting Politics? Parliament, the Public and the Internet', *Parliamentary Affairs*, 59/1 (2006), p. 28.
15. See Zittel, 'Political Representation in the Networked Society: The Americanisation of European Systems of Responsible Party Government', p. 47.
16. See Zittel, 'Political Representation in the Networked Society: The Americanisation of European Systems of Responsible Party Government', p. 50.
17. See Zittel, 'Political Representation in the Networked Society: The Americanisation of European Systems of Responsible Party Government', p. 50.
18. See Zittel, 'Political Representation in the Networked Society: The Americanisation of European Systems of Responsible Party Government', p. 44.
19. See Zittel, 'Electronic Democracy and Electronic Parliaments: A Comparison between the US House, the Swedish Riksdagen and the German Bundestag', p. 8.
20. See Lusoli, Ward and Gibson, '(Re)connecting Politics? Parliament, the Public and the Internet', p. 35.
21. In July 2006, the web address for this was http://www.tasso.nu.
22. See Zittel, 'Political Representation in the Networked Society: The Americanisation of European Systems of Responsible Party Government', p. 48.
23. Taken from an interview with Tobias Billström, Moderate Party MP.
24. Taken from an interview with Berit Högman, SAP member.
25. Taken from an interview with Crister Winbäck, Liberal MP.
26. See Zittel, 'Electronic Democracy and Electronic Parliaments: A Comparison between the US House, the Swedish Riksdagen and the German Bundestag', p. 10.
27. See Lusoli, Ward and Gibson, '(Re)connecting Politics? Parliament, the Public and the Internet', p. 28.
28. Ward and Vedel, 'Introduction: The Potential of the Internet Revisited', p. 213.
29. P. Norris, 'Preaching to the Converted? Pluralism, Participation and Party Websites', *Party Politics*, 9/1 (2003), pp. 21–46.
30. Taken from an interview with Carl B. Hamilton, Liberal Party MP.
31. A 'political blog' is defined here, using the definition first proposed by Ferguson and Griffths – namely 'as weblogs on which the content focuses on issues, events and policy in a constituency, national, international or party political context' – see R. Ferguson and B. Griffiths, 'Thin Democracy? Parliamentarians, Citizens and the Influence of Blogging on Political Engagement', *Parliamentary Affairs*, 59/2 (2006), p. 366.
32. Figures for both the SAP and Moderate Party websites calculated on 20 July 2006.
33. Indeed, 2006 may represent a potentially important chronological shift in terms of Swedish politics generally; the launch of the political blog of leading politician Margot Wallström (in autumn 2005), in anticipation of the 2006 General Election, attracted considerable attention from the Swedish media.
34. Quoted in C. M. Fagerholm, 'Bloggarna tar in skvallret i politiken' [Blogging takes gossip into politics], *Aftonbladet*, 19 May 2006.
35. Taken from an interview with Carl B. Hamilton, Liberal Party MP.
36. Lusoli, Ward and Gibson, '(Re)connecting Politics? Parliament, the Public and the Internet', p. 40.

37. Lusoli, Ward and Gibson, '(Re)connecting Politics? Parliament, the Public and the Internet', p. 40.
38. P. Esaiasson and S. Holmberg, *Representation From Above. Members of Parliament and Representative Democracy in Sweden* (Aldershot: Dartmouth, 1996), p. 310.
39. O. Petersson, K. von Beyme, L. Karvonen, B. Nedelmann and E. Smith, *Democracy: the Swedish Way, Report From the Democratic Audit of Sweden*, (Stockholm: SNS Förlag, 1999), p. 120.
40. R. Allan, 'Parliament, Elected Representatives and Technology 1997–2005 – Good in Parts', *Parliamentary Affairs*, 59/2 (2006), p. 362.
41. N. Jackson, 'An MP's Role in the Internet Era – The Impact of E-newsletters', *Journal of Legislative Studies*, 12/2 (2006), p. 237.
42. T. Nandorf, 'Högkvarteret skall få lektion i valetik' [Headquarters shall get a lesson in election-ethics], *Dagens Nyheter*, 28 February 2006.
43. R. Triches, 'Fp-bloggar påstås ligga bakom rykten' [Liberal Party's blogs assumed as responsible for the spreading of rumours], *Aftonbladet*, 18 May 2006.
44. See O. Nilsson, 'Fp tillsätter valanalys-grupp' [Liberal Party (Folkpartiet) appoints an election analysis group], *Göteborgs–Posten*, 21 September 2006.
45. Ward and Vedel, 'Introduction: The Potential of the Internet Revisited', p. 217.
46. See Allan, 'Parliament, Elected Representatives and Technology 1997–2005 – Good in Parts', p. 361.
47. Taken from interviews with Margareta Brundin and Anna Olderius, IT Department, Riksdag.
48. See Riktlinjer för användning av Internet och elektronisk post (e-post) vid datorer anslutna till riksdagsförvaltningens nätverk [Guidelines for the use of Internet and email at computers connected on the Riksdag's administrative network] (14 June 2000), and Riksdagens IT-strategi [The Riksdag's IT-strategy], available from the Swedish Riskdag, Stockholm (1 March 2003).

III. PARLIAMENTARY e-DEMOCRACY: COMPARATIVE ANALYSIS

Websites of Parliamentarians across Europe

Mª ROSA VICENTE-MERINO

The study of the effects of Information and Communication Technologies (ICTs), and in particular the Internet, on political systems is becoming an important field of research within contemporary political science. What started in the early 1990s as mainly a highly speculative debate has developed into a rigorous and ever-growing area of study within which empirical investigations are flourishing. Although a group of authors has argued that the spread of new media is not making much of a difference in the distribution of power in the political world,[1] many others have documented – in various forms and with different conclusions – that new ICTs are indeed transforming the way political processes take place in our societies. It is expected that with the further development and spread of the Internet, this impact can only become stronger. The discussion nowadays is, therefore, not so much about *whether* there is an impact, but rather, about *in what ways* the process takes place.[2] Thus, the aim for Internet scholars today is not so much to discuss whether new ICTs affect or not the way democracy works, but rather to analyse *concrete* developments introduced by the new media. For this it makes sense to focus on how specific actors are using ICTs and how political and social practices are being affected, rather than attempting to provide bold, global explanations about the effects of new media on democracy in general. This article analyses how a particular application of the Internet, the World Wide Web (WWW), is being used by European parliamentarians as part of their functions as legislators, scrutinisers and, mainly, representatives. Concretely, the research focuses on the use, and non-use, of personal websites by members from four different parliaments: the British, the European, the Portuguese, and the Swedish parliaments.

This article investigates two main research questions: 1) How many European parliamentarians are making use of personal websites for their parliamentary work? 2) How are the parliamentarians' websites being used, and, what is the *content* of these websites in terms of interactivity? Both these questions will be addressed from a *comparative* perspective, incorporating into the research, data from the four countries that constitute the case studies of this work.

The *attitudes* expressed by the MPs themselves towards the use of the Web for their parliamentary work will be taken into account in the analysis of this data. On a more theoretical note, the necessity – or not – for parliamentarians to develop very sophisticated websites will be discussed.

A variety of methods were used to gather the data upon which this research is based.[3] First of all, *web surveys* were undertaken – in some cases more than once – at different times between September 2004 and August 2006. These surveys were structured on two levels: at the first level, we looked at the generic website of each parliament; after this, those individual websites of the parliamentarians that were *linked to* the parliament's site were analysed. The former provided the researcher with data referring to the *proportion of MPs* with websites,[4] the latter provided data referring to the *content* of MPs' personal websites, from which conclusions could be drawn about the functions and uses of such websites. The *content analysis* of these individual websites focused on the participatory and linkage opportunities made available in each site. This analysis was undertaken using the software for statistical analysis SPSS. On the participatory side, the number of interactive elements were counted and codified into a '*Scale of Interactivity*'.[5] Secondly, as quantitative data about attitudes from European MPs towards the use of ICTs is scarce, due to parliamentarians throughout Europe being traditionally resistant to participation in this type of research,[6] the results of our own questionnaire surveys conducted during March – May 2005 with all members of the four parliaments will be described and analysed in this work. Finally, these data will be complemented with the results that we obtained from personal interviews with parliamentarians and parliamentary staff.

PROPORTION OF MPS WITH WEBSITES

Proportion of MPs with Personal Websites

Whatever the intentions for going online, many parliamentarians across Europe have started to develop a presence on the Web by establishing individual websites. In this section, the proportion of MPs with personal websites linked to their correspondent parliament's website is analysed from within a comparative perspective, taking into account institutional differences between the four parliaments as well as other individual factors from parliamentarians such as gender or age that might affect this proportion.

Earlier studies on this area have shown a strong variance in the proportion of MPs with personal websites in different countries. Outside Europe, the rates vary from 52 per cent found for Australian MPs[7] to over 98 per cent for US parliamentarians, found by Zittel.[8] Within Europe, our own data show that almost three quarters of Swedish MPs and considerably more than half British MPs have personal websites, whereas no Portuguese MP had a link to a personal website from the parliament's portal, and less than half of

TABLE 1
PROPORTION OF PERSONAL WEBSITES FROM MPS LINKED TO EACH PARLIAMENT

Parliament	British	European	Swedish	Portuguese
Total number of MPs in parliament	2004 : 659 2006 : 646	2004 : 732 2006 : 731	364	230
Number of personal websites from MPs *linked* to the parliament's site	2004 : 430 2006 : 431	2004 : 192 2006 : 316	255	–
Percentage of MPs with personal websites *linked* to the parliament's site	2004 : 65.2 2006 : 66.7	2004 : 27.8 2006 : 43.2	70.1	0.0

Note: For the British and European parliaments, two different surveys were undertaken, one in 2004 and a second in 2006.

MEPs did so (See Table 1). From a total of 241 MPs who responded to our questionnaires, 163 (67.6 per cent) replied that they had a personal website. By country, 81.4 per cent of Swedish MPs, 81.4 per cent of British MPs, 83.3 per cent of MEPs and 17.4 per cent of Portuguese MPs, reported having an individual website. The higher proportion of MPs reporting in having a personal website compared with our findings might be explained by the different perceptions from parliamentarians regarding what a personal website is. They may be referring to campaign sites or blogs, or even to just a page within a broader party or parliamentary group site. For our survey, we only took into account those *individual* websites linked to the parliamentary site.

From within our cases, Swedish MPs are the ones who are establishing a web presence at the highest rate: over 70 per cent of Swedish parliamentarians have a personal website linked to their parliament's website. Having parliamentarians who make most use of the new media seems to be in line with the expectation of a country with high Internet penetration. The percentage is also considerably higher than that found by Zittel[9] of 28.6 per cent for the same parliament, and it might show a growing perception among Swedish MPs that, to be a politician nowadays, one needs to establish a web presence, an idea that kept reappearing in our interviews with Swedish parliamentarians.

Contrary to what could be expected, two years and a general election have not made much difference in the proportion of British MPs with individual websites linked to parliament.uk – in 2004, 65.2 per cent of British MPs had a personal website linked to the parliament's site, while in 2006, this percentage only rose to 66.7 per cent. These findings are in line with the previous studies in the area: in 2002, Coleman and Spiller found that 67 per cent of MPs of the ones who responded to their survey had a website.[10] Similarly, in 2003, Ward and Lusoli found that 71 per cent of British MPs had websites, although only 42 per cent were coded by the authors as working ones in their analysis.[11] On the other hand, it shows a good improvement from the low rate of 28 per cent of MPs with accessible sites in March 2002 found by Jackson.[12]

On the other hand, these two years do seem to have made a strong difference in the proportion of Members of the European Parliament with an individual website. Whereas, in 2004, just over a quarter (27.8 per cent) of MEPs had a website linked to the 'europarl' portal; in 2006, this proportion had almost doubled (43.2 per cent). The trend seems to confirm the attitude of MEPs towards the increasing use of ICT to establish a relationship with those they represent in the specific context of a parliament that has been accused of being too remote from its constituents. At the moment, however, the fact that more than half of these MEPs are not directing citizens towards individual websites reveals that the tendency is far from widespread yet.

Finally, no Portuguese MP had a personal website linked to their parliament's portal. This may be explained by a variety of reasons. On the one hand, Portugal has the lowest rates of Internet penetration from within our case studies.[13] Also, as already noted by Cristina Leston-Bandeira, the Portuguese parliament is mainly organised around PGs instead of individual MPs. This means that, as we learnt from our interviews, Portuguese MPs get less individual support in terms of staff and resources from parliament than other MPs. With fewer financial resources and less staff support, it can hardly be expected that these parliamentarians can find the time to maintain a website.[14] Many of our interviewees confirmed this point; as one Portuguese parliamentarian told us: 'MPs don't have the means to have a personal website. I may have the help of the Central Services of Informatics (at the parliament) but then I am the one who has to upload it and maintain it.'[15] The rest of our interviewees corroborated this same view: 'I don't believe that an MP has the time to keep something like that. They would have to have a team to keep it going.'[16] and also: 'I don't have a personal website because I don't have the time to do it or the money to pay someone to do it.'[17]

In addition, because of the nature of the electoral system, purely proportional, it makes sense to think that a citizen who wants to find information or communicate with his or her representative would turn to a party's website, rather than to one from an individual parliamentarian – a point that was also suggested by several of our interviewees. This may have made the webmasters of the parliament's portal think that there was no need to include any link to an individual MP's website from within that portal. However, we also found from our interviews that the Internet, particularly email up to now, may be contributing towards a more personalised relationship between the represented and individual representatives, and in this sense, it can be expected in the future that Portuguese MPs will develop more personal websites. In the European Parliament's website, three Portuguese MEPs did offer a link to a personal website, out of a total of 24.

Which MPs are Building Up Websites? Differences between Parties and Countries

At a first glance, *party* does not seem to matter much. This finding falls in line with those from previous studies such as Jackson's for British MPs[18] and Chappelet's[19] for Swiss MPs. However, other scholars have found parties to be a good predictor of the probabilities of MPs having a web presence. In particular, and in the British context, Liberal Democrat parliamentarians have consistently shown more probability of setting up a website than MPs from other parties.[20] Our survey of the British parliament in 2006, which is analysed in the article by Philip Norton, shows that indeed a higher rate of Liberal Democrat MPs have a website (77.4 per cent) than MPs from Labour (66.5 per cent) or Conservative (69.3 per cent) parties. The scenario at the European Parliament is a different one, as discussed in Xiudian Dai's article in this volume. Here, it is the Group of the Greens with the highest proportion of MEPs linked to individual websites (57.2 per cent), followed closely by the Liberal Democrat group (55.0 per cent) and, with much lower rates, the European People's Party (47.5 per cent) and the Socialist group (36.3 per cent). Thus the so-called 'Liberal Democrat effect'[21] seems to be confirmed in the British context, but not so much in other parliaments.

On the other hand, however, the differences between the other parties are small. Following the 'Equalisation Thesis' in Internet studies, which argues that smaller parties find more incentives to go online, and thus will develop more and have more sophisticated websites, we would expect parliamentarians from smaller parties to have a higher presence on the Web than those from the big parties. This is not the case. Although there are exceptions (in the British case, the only party where all the MPs had set up a website was a small one, the Ulster Unionists; in the European parliament, as we have seen, the Greens are the group with the highest proportion of MEPs with individual websites), in general, our findings do not show such a trend. However, one needs to take into account that smaller parties may indeed be developing stronger party websites than bigger ones, something that this research does not look at, as its focus is only on individual parliamentarians' websites.

In the case of the European Parliament, it is worth noticing the differences between *countries* on the MEPs' proportion of websites linked to the europarl portal. These have changed considerably since 2004. In that year, only 2.6 per cent of French MEPs showed a link to a personal website. The proportion in 2006 has risen to 20.5 per cent. The lowest rate belongs to Spain: in 2004, 3.7 per cent of Spanish MEPs had a link to an individual site in the portal; in 2006, this number had risen to 9.3 per cent, the lowest proportion among the 25 countries of the European Parliament. The country with the highest proportions of MEPs with a personal website is, in 2006, Slovenia (100.0 per cent), followed by Denmark (85.7 per cent) and Finland (78.6 per cent). An unexpected finding is that of Swedish MEPs: only 47.4 per cent of them had a personal website linked to the europarl portal in November 2004 (52.7 per cent in August 2006). This is considerably lower than the proportion of Swedish MPs with a personal website linked to the Riksdagen portal on roughly the same date, which, as we have seen, is over 70 per cent. In the British case, also, a lower proportion of MEPs have websites (46.2 per cent) than British MPs (66.7 per cent).

CONTENT OF MPS' WEBSITES

What are Parliamentarians' Websites used for? Interactivity

Interactivity is one of the most important features of those that distinguish the Internet from other media. Unlike other forms of communication, where the information can only go from one source to the other in a top-down, one-directional sense, the use of interactive elements in websites allows for a bottom-up style of communication. This can lead to a change in power relations, because the insider/outsider dichotomy in the communication process can be overcome.[22] Through the use of interactive elements in MPs' websites, citizens and parliamentarians are, therefore, able to establish a less hierarchical relationship, which can in turn enhance the interest and participation from individuals in their communication with representatives.

Moreover, a website can only have as many interactive elements as the person responsible for the site wants; if one particular site has a high degree of interactivity, there is an intention behind this. It can be argued that MPs with websites who make the most of the interactive – and also of the linking – features of the Web are intentionally trying to explore new possibilities for communication and relationships with their constituents. On the other hand, a website where not even email contact details for the MP are provided is sending the clear message that the parliamentarian is using the Web only as another one-way, top-down, tool for information and publicity. These observations will be further discussed below. Before this, the results of our web surveys regarding the *content* of individual MPs' websites is explored.

Parliamentarians' websites across Europe *are not very interactive*. Only a small minority of MPs have introduced elements in their websites that allow for a high degree of interactivity between user and producer. When all the individual websites from parliamentarians were analysed and subsequently coded, we found that in all three cases (British, European and Swedish parliaments) the vast majority of MPs' websites fell into the 'Very Low' or 'Low' categories in our *Scale of Interactivity*. Concretely, 83.0 per cent of British MPs' websites analysed, 75.5 per cent of MEPs' (79.2 per cent in 2004) and 86.7 per cent of Swedish MPs' had none, very low or low interactivity (see Table 2).

Swedish MPs' websites seem to be less interactive, compared with members of the British and European parliaments. As we can see, they have the highest proportion of websites in the 'Very low' category, whereas MEPs have the most interactive sites, with the highest rates both in the 'Very high' and 'High' fields. This finding might be in line with our hypothesis about financial resources and staff support ascribed to an MP being of very high relevance for the development of this parliamentarian's web presence. Swedish MPs have no individual staff support ascribed to

TABLE 2
SCALE OF INTERACTIVITY ACROSS PARLIAMENTARIANS' WEBSITES(%)

MPs' Websites Scale of Interactivity	British	European	Swedish	Portuguese
None	4.9 (21)	2004:– 2006: 1.6 (5)	–	–
Very Low	60.7 (261)	2004 : 55.2 (106) 2006 : 55.0 (169)	79.6 (203)	–
Low	17.4 (75)	2004 : 24.0 (46) 2006 : 20.5 (63)	7.1 (18)	–
Medium	4.0 (17)	2004 : 3.1 (6) 2006 : 3.3 (10)	–	–
High	4.0 (17)	2004 : 7.3 (14) 2006 : 3.6 (11)	1.6 (4)	–
Very High	4.4 (19)	2004 : 8.3 (16) 2006 : 16.0 (49)	3.1 (8)	–
Missing	4.7 (20)	2004 : 2.1 (4) 2006 : 2.8 (9)	8.6 (22)	–
TOTAL	100 (430)	2004 : 100 (192) 2006 : 100 (316)	100 (255)	–

Note: i) Missing values correspond to links that did not work or websites under construction. ii) There are no values for the Portuguese parliament column as no Portuguese MP had a personal website linked from the parliament's portal.

them personally in their parliament. Both members of the British and the European parliaments have not only one, but several assistants working directly for them. As we found in our interviews, typically one of these members of staff will be in charge of the MP's website: updating it regularly, and generally taking care of it. In our interviews, Swedish MPs showed interest, though also caution, in the most innovative features available on the Web, but they might be simply lacking the time and resources to include those in their personal websites, which they generally maintain and take care of personally. As one of our interviewees – a member from the Swedish parliament – puts it: 'If I have a website I would have to take care of it myself and maybe then I won't have the time to go out and talk to people, that sort of thing worries very much'.[23]

In our conversations, Swedish parliamentarians were the group that showed most scepticism about the value of including interactive elements such as messageboards in their websites. Most of our interviewees had had bad experiences with online deliberation, which created some doubt that real political debate can ever take place in a digital form. For instance, one MP told us that 'the [online] discussion fora are very difficult: either there is very little debate, or much debate but bad debate. It's hard to get serious continuous debate.'[24] We will come back to this point later in this article but for the moment it is worth keeping in mind that this is a possible explanation for the low level of interactivity displayed in these MPs' websites.

The level of interactivity in parliamentarians' websites is, in any case, generally low for *all the cases* of our study. Only 1.2 per cent of all websites analysed for the British parliament had an online forum or messageboard. The case of blogs is an interesting one. This feature has attracted considerable attention from the media about its possible uses for political purposes. Whereas the percentages of MPs' websites with a blog is quite low (below four per cent in most cases) in the European Parliament context it is worth noting that, while in 2004 only 2.7 per cent of MEPs' personal websites included a blog, this percentage had risen to 9.1 per cent in 2006. Most of the parliamentarians who were interviewed for this research were considering the possibility of setting up a blog in the near future. In the Swedish context, for instance, the upcoming elections are expected to make a strong difference in the number of parliamentarians engaged in online discussions via blogs.

Why are parliamentarians not making the most of the interactive capabilities of the new media? On the very practical level, MPs might simply lack the time to maintain a highly interactive website. Moreover, even if they can afford staff to take care of updating their websites, if the MP themselves do not have the time to learn about the new possibilities for communication allowed by the Internet, then it is doubtful that they would be interested in setting up a sophisticated site.

From our questionnaires we also found that MPs seem to want to use their websites more as tools to offer information, rather than to communicate or to get feedback: 79.1 per cent of the parliamentarians who replied to our question about the purpose of their website told us that 'offering information about his or her work' was the most relevant function. Only 27.2 per cent said that 'getting feedback from constituents' was the 'most relevant' purpose of their personal websites. This was also confirmed in our interviews: most of the parliamentarians interviewed for this study who had personal websites told us that their main function was the delivery of information directly to their constituents.

Finally, the possibility of communicating with a *targeted audience*, a selected group of interested citizens, through the use of newsletters or mailing lists was also highly appreciated by our interviewees, which explains why these elements seem to be popular among MPs' websites (see Table 3). Talking about her personal homepage, a member of the European Parliament told us that with her newsletter, sent out once a month, she does 'not try to give the general views, they can get the general views from other places, can't they?... It's a very focused [newsletter] with a very focused group in mind.... It's quite a good tool to achieve very specialised focused groups, not the general public.'[25]

TABLE 3
INTERACTIVE ELEMENTS ACROSS PARLIAMENTARIANS' WEBSITES (%)

MPs' Websites Elements	British	European	Swedish	Portuguese
E-Mail contact	93.4 (2004 Survey: 97.0)	2004 : 98.9 2006 : 97.7	97.4	–
Email list or newsletter	35.6 (2004 Survey: 28.0)	2004 : 33.5 2006 : 26.1	9.9	–
Online surgery	1.9	–	–	–
Online poll or survey	6.3	2004 : 5.3 2006 : 5.5	1.7	–
Online guestbook	1.7	2004 : 5.9 2006 : 4.9	3.0	–
Online petitions	2.4	2004 : 2.1 2006 : 0.7	0.0	–
Messageboard or forum	1.2	2004 : 5.9 2006 : 7.5	2.6	–
Blog	3.7	2004 : 2.7 2006 : 9.1	0.9	–

Note: All values for British MPs' websites correspond to the most recent data from the survey undertaken in March 2006, unless otherwise stated.
Also note that for this table missing values (broken links or websites that did not work) were not taken into account.

WHY SHOULD MPs BUILD HIGHLY SOPHISTICATED WEBSITES?

A point that became clear during our conversations with parliamentarians was the feeling that they *need to have a website*. As a member of the European Parliament put it, 'You must have a website. All MEPs feel the need to have it.'[26] To be a politician nowadays, it requires to be engaged with the new media, or at least to be seen as such by citizens and journalists. Websites in this sense can, and are, used as another instrument of political marketing in these times of 'permanent campaign'. Beyond electoral motives, however, why should representatives spend time and effort setting up sophisticated homepages?

Parliamentarians may choose to establish a web presence for a variety of reasons. Through a website, an MP can offer information *directly* to the public, without the mediation of external agents such as journalists. A parliamentarian on the Web can therefore, *bypass traditional news media filters* to connect directly with the electorate[27] – a possibility, which makes a website very attractive for members of parliament as a tool for campaign and electoral purposes.[28] *Peer pressure* can also drive an MP to build up a website. Typically, in any given organisation the turn towards ICT would be started by a small group of pioneers and the rest would follow. The same applies for the parliamentary environment, where, as it was confirmed by our interviews, the few enthusiastic MPs who make an intense use of digital technologies act not only as pioneers, but also as trendsetters among their colleagues.[29] The necessity to be seen as up-to-date in terms of technology, particularly among members from old institutions such as parliaments in established democracies, might also drive parliamentarians to set up a web presence. One of our interviewees, from a Conservative background – a party stereotyped sometimes as 'out of date' and 'old fashioned'– confirmed that a website has become nowadays 'something you should be able to say you have, to prove that even conservatives do technology'.[30] More specifically, parliamentarians may decide to build up their own website 'basically to shut people up when they ask whether I have a website',[31] as another member of the European Parliament put it in one of our interviews.

If many parliamentarians are willing to accept that they maintain a personal website mainly because it is something that has to be had, then why is there such a strong tendency – popular nowadays both within academic circles and the media – to assume that all parliamentarians *should* have highly sophisticated websites. In this section, a few of the problems with this trend will be outlined. The intention is not to give an extensive account of these arguments, but rather to draw attention to the objections that can be made to the view that having complex websites is *only good* for MPs, and thus to set some of the grounds for discussion on this topic.

Politicians Versus Celebrities

In the age of reality television and political disenchantment, the pressure for public figures to become *performers* can arise. This development can be strengthened by the Internet and, in particular, personal websites. What is the need for a parliamentarian to set up a blog in his or her homepage where comments about what film he or she watched last night or where lunch would be taken today are updated daily? Moreover, is there a risk of politicians becoming celebrities – or wanting to become so – while at the same time failing to fulfil other public functions and responsibilities? Can they be both? In an MEP's words: 'Are politicians performers or representatives? Is the Internet destructing, rather than helping?'.[32]

We have seen that parliamentarians use their websites mainly as tools for the direct transmission of information about themselves and their work. They seem to be far less interested in the communicative aspects of the Web or on the possibility of listening to the feedback from constituents, as we learnt from our questionnaires. Used as media through which to reach people directly, websites can easily become mere exercises of individualism. The danger is not only that MPs seem to be neglecting to use the interactive and networking capabilities of the Internet, but that they actually may be using the new media to enhance the 'individualisation and *celebritisation* of representatives'.

On the other hand, through new digital technologies parliamentarians may be able to reach a segment of society traditionally perceived as unengaged and disinterested in politics: the youth. In our interviews, most MPs showed an interest in the possibilities that innovative uses of the Internet might attract younger citizens into politics. If using a blog, even in a frivolous manner, makes a parliamentarian better known with the younger generation, this can be a step towards the final goal of making the 'old, boring politics' attractive to the young. What is more, for an ever-increasing digitalised youth, representatives who fail to use the technologies in an innovative way may be seen out of touch with their reality, and thus the gap between them might only just grow. We should not forget, however, that some responsibility is needed by politicians when using their personal websites to engage citizens. Setting up a highly sophisticated website, with a daily updated blog, a couple of online polls, and a digital messageboard might help an MP to become more visible within the younger section of his or her constituency, and thus gain some more votes. Real engagement can only come through genuine opportunities for participation and communication within these websites. This leads to our next question: are interactive elements truly promoting authentic channels for political participation?

Problems with Interactivity Online: Is Deliberation Possible Online? Are Digital Surveys Truly Representative?

One of the most common claims of those who see in the development of new ICTs an opportunity for enhancing participation in contemporary democracies is that, through the new technologies everyone has, at least potentially, the opportunity to have a voice and be heard. For instance, through online political consultation, representatives could give citizens the opportunity to express their opinions on a specific policy and these opinions be taken into account in the decision-making process. The same can be said for digital surveys or online messageboards: they all provide the means by which the people's voice could be heard by politicians. Most of our interviewees are aware of these possibilities. However, they also raised questions about the validity of these instruments for enhancing meaningful political participation.

First, there are the problems connected with *access* and *representativity*. Studies keep showing that the Internet so far has failed to attract more citizens into the political processes, and instead is repeating a 'virtuous circle' of political activism in which the already engaged and politically active are the ones using the new technologies in a political way.[33] This thesis was shared by some of our interviewees; as one put it, 'I think that websites are very important, but not as important as other media to get into people... Particularly people who aren't interested in what you have got to say. The only people likely to access your website are people who are already interested in the MP.'[34] On the other hand, Norris herself acknowledged in a later study that the Internet is indeed expanding the numbers of the politically active, as it reaches to groups typically less active in conventional forms of politics, that is, the younger generations.[35]

In addition, scholars, journalists and also some of our interviewees, have raised questions about the possibilities for *real deliberation* taking place in an online format. Some fear that the problem is the *anonymity* in these fora, which *depersonalises* the discussion and allows some individuals to use abusive or plain insulting language; others the *speed* at which communication takes place within them, which neglects the chance of reflection before forming an opinion. In any case, the view by many is that users of these messageboards often seem to be more interested in *reinforcing* their own ideas than in listening to what others have to say, and thus the possibilities for debate are lost. These problems have been discussed extensively in academic circles[36] and, again, need to be dealt with before assuming that a website with an online forum is necessarily 'more democratic' than one without.

What Do Citizens Want?

So far, we have considered the attitudes of parliamentarians towards the use of websites for strengthening their relationship with the represented. We have also discussed the problems about the instruments that were usually perceived as having the potential for the development of this relationship. In this section, we look at these questions from another point of view – , that of the citizen. It has commonly been assumed by some groups of scholars that if large segments of the population are not participating in politics nowadays this is because they do not find channels through which to do it. Taking this view, citizens will be most willing to make use of any online instrument that allows them to participate.

Surveys, however, have shown that citizens are not really *that interested* in the most interactive elements available in political websites. In a study of visitors to political websites, Boogers and Voerman found that in the few cases where political websites in the Dutch parliamentary elections of 2002 offered opportunities for two-way communication, these were hardly taken up by the citizens visiting the sites.[37] In the UK context, Ward, Gibson and Lusoli write that, based on a NOP Survey from 2004, citizens appreciate elements that strengthen the one-to-one relation between representative and represented, but they do not show much appreciation of elements that contribute to ongoing relations such as online fora.[38]

With these findings in mind, why should parliamentarians build up sophisticated websites? It could be claimed that there is no need for this, if citizens are not really interested in the interactive and networking possibilities of the Web. This argument, however, is not without problems. First, citizens may not be interested *just yet*. It takes a period of time to get used to new technologies and to the new ways of communication that are introduced to them, and thus it takes time to be able to make the most of these new channels and to learn how to use them for meaningful participation. This also applies, of course, to the other side, the parliamentarians' side. Second, visitors of political websites may not take part in the mechanisms for two-way communication because they perceive that these channels are not really taken that seriously by the political actors behind the websites. If there is an online messageboard in a parliamentarian's website but one can see that the MP never posts in it or replies to any questions posed, why would a citizen bother to contribute to a debate that most probably will not be taken into account by the MP? Until there is a perception that politicians are making a sincere and responsible use (beyond mere electoral motives) of these opportunities for participation and communication with those they represent, we can expect that a lot of citizens will simply not bother to look at the elements available.

CONCLUSION

Parliamentarians across Europe differ in their use of the Internet as a tool for their parliamentary work. From a comparative point of view, a number of institutional and political factors play a role in both the *proportion* of MPs with personal websites and the *content* of these sites. On the other hand, in general, European parliamentarians *are not* making use of the most innovative features of the Internet, particularly its possibilities for interactivity and networking. They consider their websites as something that 'has to be had', using them mainly as a device to offer information about themselves and less as a mechanism through which to communicate with or get feedback from their constituents. It has to be kept in mind, nevertheless, that the Internet has been around only for a short time, and that this scenario is likely to change as the newer generations, more familiarised with the digital media, become older.

Regarding the *proportion* of parliamentarians with personal websites, we found that from our four cases, Swedish MPs are the ones who are most established on the Web. At the other side of the spectrum, Portuguese MPs seemed to be the least 'digitalised'. A number of 'offline factors' have been suggested as offering plausible explanations for these differences, including; 1) rate of Internet penetration within the society (in parliaments with higher rates, more MPs have personal websites); 2) organisation of Parliament (in those where parliamentary groups have a stronger presence, fewer MPs will set up individual sites); 3) level of financial and staff support to the MP (the lower this support, the less likely an MP will be to establish an online presence) and 4) nature of the electoral system (those MPs from proportional systems will be less interested in establishing an individualised relationship with citizens).

In terms of the *content* of these personal websites, Swedish MPs had less interactive websites than those from members of the British and the European

Parliament. This can be explained by the lower level of financial and staff support offered to Swedish parliamentarians, which supports our thesis about the strong influence of 'offline factors' in the behaviour of political actors, and in particular parliamentarians, on the Net. In any case, the majority of websites analysed from *all cases* showed a *low degree of interactivity*. Why are parliamentarians not making their websites interactive? Lack of time and interest, in combination with the function that parliamentarians *want* to ascribe to their websites (as vehicles to offer information rather than to communicate) are explanations to consider here.

NOTES

1. See for instance: M. Margolis and D. Resnick, *Politics as Usual: the Cyberspace 'Revolution'*, (Thousand Oaks, (CA): Sage, 2001).
2. See, among others: S. Coleman, J. A. Taylor, and W. van de Donk, 'Introduction', in S. Coleman, J. A. Taylor and W. van de Donk (eds.), *Parliaments in the Age of the Internet* (Oxford: Oxford University Press, 1999), A. Chadwick, *Internet Politics. States, Citizens, and New Communications Technologies* (New York and Oxford: Oxford University Press, 2006).
3. For other methodological issues see the introductory article in this special issue or the appendices, available at the request from the author of this article at mrosavicentemerino@gmail.com
4. Only those personal websites to which *links* were found at the relevant section ('Directory of Members') of each of the four parliaments' sites were taken into account in our study. If a member of parliament had a personal website but this was not linked to his/her parliamentary website, then it was not taken into account.
5. The scale characterised websites according to their degree of interactivity, from those with 'none' interactivity (no interactive elements at all) to 'very high' sites (those which included an online forum or a blog). Concretely, those websites where no interactive elements were found, not even an email address for contact, were considered as having 'none' interactivity. Those websites with 'very low' interactivity are those in which the visitor could contact the parliamentarian or his/her web/staff team via an online form or an email address. Websites with 'low' interactivity are those which also included the possibility to subscribe to an online bulletin, email list or newsletter, and in the British case the possibility of an online surgery. Those with 'medium' offered the possibility to take part in an online poll or survey (with close answers). In the websites classified as having 'high' interactivity visitors could express their opinions via online guestbooks. Finally, in those websites with 'very high' interactivity real possibilities for interactive communication were available through either a blog, an online forum or messageboard, or both.
6. J. Hoff, 'Members of Parliaments' Use of ICT in a Comparative European Perspective' *Information Polity*, 9/1–2 (2004), pp. 5–16.
7. R. K. Gibson, W. Lusoli, and S. Ward, 'Phile or Phobe? Australian and British MPs and the New Communication Technology', paper prepared for the 100th Annual Meeting of the American Political Science Association, Chicago, 31 August–4 September 2004.
8. T. Zittel, 'Political Representation in the Networked Society: The Americanisation of European Systems of Responsible Party Government?' *Journal of Legislative Studies*, 9/3 (2003), pp. 32–53.
9. Zittel, 'Political Representation in the Networked Society: The Americanisation of European Systems of Responsible Party Government?'
10. S. Coleman and J. Spiller, 'Exploring New Media Effects on Representative Democracy' *Journal of Legislative Studies*, 9/3 (2003), pp. 1–16.

11. S. Ward and W. Lusoli, '"From Weird to Wired": MPs, the Internet and Representative Politics in the UK', *Journal of Legislative Studies*,11/1 (2005), pp. 57–81.

12. N. Jackson, 'MPs and Web Technologies: an Untapped Opportunity?' *Journal of Public Affairs*, 3/29 (2003), pp. 124–37.

13. The most up-to-date data available (31st March 2006, 'European Union Internet Usage Stats and Population Statistics, available at, http://www.internetworldstats.com; retrieved July 2006) shows the following rates of Internet penetration (percentage of the population): Portugal, 58.0 per cent, Sweden, 74.9 per cent, United Kingdom, 62.9 per cent.

14. On the other hand, Swedish MPs also have a lower level of staff support than British ones or MEPs, yet most of them have set up websites. Perhaps they get more financial resources individually.

15. Member of the Portuguese parliament, interviewed on 23 June 2005.

16. Member of the Portuguese parliament (21 June 2005).

17. Member of the Portuguese parliament (22 June 2005).

18. Jackson, 'MPs and Web Technologies: an Untapped Opportunity?'

19. J. L. Chappelet, 'The Appropriation of E-Mail and the Internet by Members of the Swiss Parliament' *Information Polity*, 9/1–2 (2004), pp. 89–102.

20. Gibson, Lusoli, and Ward, 'Phile or Phobe? Australian and British MPs and the New Communication Technology', Ward and Lusoli, 'From Weird to Wired': MPs, the Internet and Representative Politics in the UK'

21. Ward and Lusoli, 'From Weird to Wired': MPs, the Internet and Representative Politics in the UK'

22. P. J. Smith and E. Smythe 'Sleepless in Seattle: Challenging the WTO in a Globalizing World', paper presented at the *Annual Meeting of the International Studies Association*, Chicago, 23rd February 2000; L. A. Kutner, 'Environmental Activism and the Internet', *Electronic Green Journal* 12 (2000). Available at: http://egj.lib.uidahho.edu/egj12/_kutner1.html (Retrieved April 2005).

23. Member of the Swedish Parliament (16 June 2005).

24. Member of the Swedish Parliament (15 June 2005).

25. Member of the European Parliament (28 June 2005).

26. Member of the European Parliament (30 June 2005).

27. S. E. Jarvis and K. Wilkerson, 'Congress on the Internet: messages on the homepages of the US house of representatives, 1996 and 2001', *Journal of Computer-Mediated Communication*, 10/2 (2005).

28. G. Cardoso, C. Cunha, and S. Nascimento, 'Ministers of Parliament and Information and Communication Technologies as a Means of Horizontal and Vertical Communication in Western Europe' *Information Polity*, 9/1–2 (2004), pp. 29–40.

29. For a similar argument, see S. Coleman and B. Nathanson, 'Learning to Live with the Internet: How European Parliamentarians Are Adapting to the Digital Age', an EPRI Report (2005), available online at, http://www.epri.org/epriknowledge/contents/Studies.php (retrieved May 2006)

30. Member of the European Parliament (30 June 2005).

31. Member of the European Parliament (07 July 2005).

32. Member of the European Parliament (12 March 2005).

33. P. Norris, D*igital Divide. Civic Engagement, Information Poverty, and the Internet Worldwide* (Cambridge: University Press, 2001), P. Norris, *Democratic Phoenix. Reinventing Political Activism* (Cambridge: University Press, 2002).

34. Member of the British Parliament (08 August 2005).

35. P. Norris and J. Curtice, 'If You Build a Political Website, Will They Come?', paper presented at the Annual Meeting of the American Political Science Association, Chicago, 31 August – 4 September 2004.

36. See among others: A. G. Wilhelm, 'Virtual Sounding Boards: How Deliberative is Online Political Discussion?', in B. N. Hague and B. D. Loader (eds.), *Digital Democracy. Discourse and Decision Making in the Information Age* (London and New York: Routledge, 2002), N. Jankowski and M. van Selm, 'The Promise and Practice of Public Debate in Cyberspace',

in K. L. Hacker and J. van Dijk (eds.), *Digital Democracy. Issues of Theory and Practice* (London: Sage, 2000), A. Ranerup, 'Online Forums as a Tool for People-Centred Governance. Experiences from Local Government in Sweden', in L. Keeble and B. D. Loader (eds.), *Community Informatics. Shaping computer-mediated social relations* (London and New York: Routledge, 2001).

37. M. Boogers and G. Voerman, 'Surfing Citizens and Floating Voters: Results of an Online Survey of Visitors to Political Web Sites during the Dutch 2002 General Elections', *Information Polity*, 8 (2003), pp. 17–27.

38. S. Ward, R. Gibson, and W. Lusoli, 'Old Politics, New Media: Parliament, the Public and the Internet', paper presented at the *Political Science Association Annual Conference*, University of Leeds (April 2005).

Political Ethics Online: Parliamentarians' Use of Email in Europe

XIUDIAN DAI

Some are concerned that, for most citizens, 'the Internet has brought far more change to their relationship with their bank or various commercial outlets and to their social life than to their relationship with government.'[1] While using the Internet as a source of information is becoming ever more popular, a recent survey shows that, in the United Kingdom, merely six per cent of Internet users reported that they had used email to contact an MP or a councillor.[2] An important question to ask here is why Internet users are making so few email contacts with politicians. Is it because citizens are less interested in making use of Internet technologies in political participation than in other fields of life? Or is it because the other end of the citizen–government relationship is not as receptive and encouraging to citizen's interaction through Internet technologies as one might assume? By focusing on the relationship between parliamentarians and email communication, which is an important aspect of Internet technologies, this article aims to investigate (1) how elected politicians in Europe consider the relevance of email to parliamentary communication; (2) to what extent European parliamentarians are making use of email; and (3) the key ethical issues raised by parliamentarians' use of email communication.

Discussions presented in this article are based mainly on data derived from a comparative study of the British, European, Portuguese and Swedish Parliament, including a questionnaire survey, content analysis of the official website of the British, European, Portuguese and Swedish Parliament and face-to-face interviews with parliamentarians and parliamentary staff.

In the next section, perceptions of European parliamentarians about email as a tool for political communication is analysed. This is followed by a reality check of the extent to which parliamentarians were prepared to make their email addresses available on the institutional website of the four case study parliaments. The paper then moves on to discuss the use of emails by parliamentarians in the four case study parliaments with a view to establishing purposes for which politicians use email and how they deal with received emails. The fourth section discusses the main ethical challenges faced by parliamentarians in Europe in their email communication. The paper ends with a few concluding remarks.

PARLIAMENTARIANS' PERCEPTION OF EMAIL COMMUNICATION

Compared to traditional ways of communication, such as letters and telephone, email has a number of advantages. For Internet users, emails are cost – effective and efficient - the transmission of emails is hardly constrained by time and space. Our questionnaire survey shows that the majority of elected politicians are convinced that emails are important to parliamentary democracy.

First, emails are convenient to use. Of the 225 parliamentarians who responded to the point about the convenience of dealing with email communication, about two thirds of them (149 or 66.2 per cent) saw this as a 'most positive' or 'positive' advantage. Indeed, emails could be read or sent by a politician from anywhere and at any time (through either a PC or mobile device). With the help of email, elected politicians are becoming less constrained by the geography of their multiple working sites and they like this new tool:

> [The Internet is] indispensable. Without the Internet I am not even able to communicate with my offices…. Because I have like a virtual office, and that can only be established through the Net. And when I send out an email, I copy it always to all people in my office whether they are based here or in Valetta. We have constant communication…. Internally we always have a group system, where we always copy the message to the group, every message, even if it is a simple yes or no reply to something, but at least you know what the other people are doing, and then particularly they know what I am saying and the instructions that I am giving.[3]

Second, in addition to being convenient for parliamentarians to deal with, emails offer an easy way of communication between parliamentarians and their constituents. One parliamentarian believed that, in terms of communication, 'you can build up a database of email addresses in your constituency and you could send your communication...you could communicate with a large number of people.'[4] It is also the view of 72.6 per cent of our 223 questionnaire respondents that 'easy to use by constituents' is another most positive or positive advantage of email communications (see Table 1).

Third, email communications can play a positive role in improving political participation among the younger generation at a time when liberal democracy is faced with the growing challenge of voter apathy. Our survey shows that more than half (53.2 per cent) of the 222 parliamentarians who commented on the issue believed that email communication has the potential to attract young people to communicate with elected politicians. One of our interviewees commented on the problem associated with the older generations of his party members who are less active in using email, compared to the younger generation: 'The other problem we have with our membership here and our supporters is that the older generation at the moment are less likely to have an Internet [or] email connection than maybe the younger generation.'[5]

TABLE 1

PARLIAMENTARIANS' VIEW: ADVANTAGES OF EMAIL COMMUNICATION

	Number of Valid respondents	Valid percentage	Cumulative percentage
Emails are convenient to deal with			
Most positive advantage	115	51.1	51.1
Positive advantage	34	15.1	66.2
Fairly positive advantage	35	15.6	81.8
Least positive advantage	41	18.2	100.0
Total	225	100.0	
Emails are easy to use by constituents			
Most positive advantage	87	39.0	39.0
Positive advantage	75	33.6	72.6
Fairly positive advantage	34	15.2	87.9
Least positive advantage	27	12.1	100.0
Total	223	100.0	
Emails can attract young people to communicate with politicians			
Most positive advantage	64	28.8	28.8
Positive advantage	54	24.3	53.2
Fairly positive advantage	58	26.1	79.3
Least positive advantage	46	20.7	100.0
Total	222	100.0	

Although emails and posted letters are different forms of communication, the vast majority of parliamentarians who participated in our study regarded the former as just as important as the latter. To many parliamentarians, the importance of emails is comparable to posted letters in terms of political communication. Among the 240 parliamentarians who gave their view on the issue, a vast majority of them, as shown in Table 2, either totally agreed or agreed that emails are as important as letters for communication with constituents (83.3 per cent), with the general public (82.1 per cent) and with interest groups (87.1 per cent).

Despite the very positive view on email communication, it is still too early to pronounce the death of posted letters. There are parliamentarians who still attach great importance to the traditional post: 'The effort to write a letter, and let's say also to copy it and to sign it and to send it, is bigger; so people would write only very important things.'[6] This is especially applicable to communication between parliamentarians and members of their constituency. One British MP cautioned e-Democracy advocates with the following remarks:

> A lot of people that I know have bought computers but they don't actually check their emails everyday. They may put their computers on once a week. Therefore an email is not always an instant method of communication. For example,…when I go back this afternoon I will be spending some time with my family, so it maybe will not be until tomorrow

TABLE 2
ARE EMAILS AS IMPORTANT AS LETTERS?

	Number of valid respondents	Valid percentage	Cumulative percentage
For communication with constituents			
Totally agree	105	43.8	43.8
Agree	95	39.6	83.3
Disagree	28	11.7	95.0
Totally disagree	12	5.0	100.0
Total	240	100.0	
For communication with members of general public			
Totally agree	99	41.3	41.3
Agree	98	40.8	82.1
Disagree	33	13.8	95.8
Totally disagree	10	4.2	100.0
Total	240	100.0	
For communication with interest groups			
Totally agree	112	46.7	46.7
Agree	97	40.4	87.1
Disagree	24	10	97.1
Totally disagree	7	2.9	100.0
Total	240	100.0	

morning that I put my computer on. So the idea that you can send someone an email and get an immediate message to them only works if it is an office situation where computers are constantly on and people are watching it.… If you are busy doing other things, then you do not get that email. And I know people who only put their computers on once every two weeks! When they first got their computers they were really very much into it but…many people who do not have broadband are rather disappointed by the speed of the Internet…it is not the best way to communicate with them.[7]

Parliamentarians' email communication is constrained by a number of factors: all parliamentarians have a very demanding diary and they cannot be expected to deal with their emails all the time; parliamentarians have a life to live off-line; not every email user checks their emails on a regular basis; high speed of Internet connection is not universally available and, finally, access computers and a link to the Internet do not necessarily mean a politician being online.

E-DEMOCRACY AT THE DISCRETION OF PARLIAMENTARIANS?

As a general trend of development, parliaments in the European Union have embarked upon a policy of making the Internet a new tool to assist their members' political communication since the 1990s. It is indeed the case that, at the European level, strengthening political participation and democratic decision-making through the use of ICTs is one of the five major objectives of the i2010 e-Government Action Plan. In tune with the new technological and policy environment, institutional support of email communication and ICT equipment has become a priority item for the parliamentary budget at parliaments such as the UK and European Parliaments.

Although email is a relatively new tool for political communication, the provision of an official email address for each parliamentarian has already become standard practice in EU countries. Institutional support of electronic communication has become a priority in the parliamentary budget of, for example, the UK and European Parliament. Figures from the European Telework Development (ETD) indicate that, by April 1999, virtually all parliamentarians from the then 15 EU Member States already had an email address, with the exception of three countries: Greece (where only 50 out of 300 parliamentarians had an email address), Italy (where 300 out of 630 parliamentarians had an email address) and Spain (for which data were not available).[8]

Universal provision of email address, however, does not necessarily mean that all parliamentarians are prepared to publicise their email address. In fact, some parliamentarians in Europe still remain unconvinced of the need to make their email address available on their respective parliamentary website. This leads to speculation that politicians and bureaucracies find e-Democracy disruptive and they do not want to engage with untried methods.[9] It is also possible that some politicians are enthusiastic in talking about the potential of ICTs to improve the democratic system but they do not wish to become practitioners of e-Democracy. UK Prime Minister Tony Blair, for example, proclaimed himself to be a moderniser but he was alleged to be one of only a handful of world leaders not hooked up to email until very recently, when he was embarrassed by an opposition MP who decided to create a free hotmail address 'for' him.[10]

By analysing the websites of the British, European, Portuguese and Swedish Parliament, we found that the majority of parliamentarians in Europe have officially published their email addresses. Swedish MPs scored the highest, with 97.8 per cent of them indicating their email contact details, followed by British MPs (82.4 per cent). In comparison, 60.8 per cent of MEPs provided email addresses on the European Parliament's website. Portuguese MPs came last with just over half of them (52.8 per cent) having published email addresses. These figures suggest that many parliamentarians in Europe have failed to live up to their rhetoric about the positive implications of electronic communication.

Meanwhile, the above figures suggest that many parliamentarians in Europe have failed to live up to their rhetoric about the positive implications of electronic communication. The relatively high proportion (47.2 per cent) of Portuguese MPs without an email contact on the Parliament website may be explained by, firstly, the fact that Portugal has one of the lowest national Internet penetration rates among EU countries. Secondly, as we have seen in Portugal, it is the political parties, rather than individual MPs, whom voters would be likely to contact in the first place. This means the level of incentive and pressure for providing an email contact in Portugal is relatively lower than elsewhere in the EU. Thirdly, the parliamentary budget in Portugal is allocated largely to Political Groups; individual MPs do not command adequate resources for hiring office staff to help with web and email management.[11] It is, however, important to bear in mind that resources alone cannot explain the full picture. For instance, a significant proportion (39.2 per cent) of MEPs do not have an email contact published, despite the fact that they are much better funded than Portuguese MPs.

Regarding the matter of whether politicians' official email address should be published on the parliament website, the discretion seems to have been left in the hands of individual parliamentarians, rather than the parliament. The British parliament provides the following explanation about MPs' email links from the parliament website:

Members have been asked to supply details of the preferred form of their names, titles and qualifications; these have been included in this list where known. Links to email and websites are also given where available. Where an email address is not available details of postal and telephone contact points are given.[12]

When asked whether UK parliamentarians are officially obliged to advertise their email address one MP said:

We are not officially advised to advertise any address [including email address]! I mean the only address that people can write to Members of the Parliament usually is the House of Commons. I mean, we have an address here which is freely available, but there's no official requirement to advertise any address.[13]

In an explanation regarding the availability of email addresses on its website, the European Parliament states that 'Email addresses are given **only** [emphasis by the European Parliament] for those MEPs who wish them to be published'.[14]

For those parliamentarians who have provided email contact(s) on the parliament website there is a difference in the types of their email addresses, as shown in Table 3. More specifically, the vast majority of Swedish parliamentarians were happy to promote their officially assigned email address with only one exception. In contrast, of the 52.8 per cent of Portuguese parliamentarians with email contacts, only 2.6 per cent adopted the official email address and the majority of them published their non-official email address. The publication of email addresses by MEPs is split between the officially assigned address (29.5 per cent) and non-official ones (22.3 per cent) with some MEPs using both (nine per cent).

On the UK Parliament website, an email link has been created for 82.4 per cent (or 532) of the 646 MPs. However, the email link is connected with a third party service provider,[15] rather than MPs' email addresses directly. In this case, details of the email addresses are not shown on the parliament's website; instead, a hyperlink on the word 'email' takes visitors to a contact page where a message could be typed and submitted to the service provider, who would then forward the email message to the recipient MPs.

It is worth noting that the email transfer system contracted by the UK Parliament 'does not permit users to send emails from "@parliament.uk" addresses' and correspondence by email 'is forwarded once a day to MPs'.[16] This implies that, first, MPs will not get instant (or real-time) communication via email–an email message to an MP will take at least a day, instead of seconds, to reach the destination. In the age of instant communication offered by email, UpMyStreet, the email forwarding service provider,

TABLE 3
PUBLICATION AND TYPES OF EMAIL ADDRESSES BY PARLIAMENTARIANS

Indication of email address	Number of parliamentarians	Valid percentage	Cumulative percentage
British Parliament			
Yes	532	82.4	82.4
No	114	17.6	100.0
Total	646	100.0	
European Parliament			
Yes–official	216	29.5	29.5
Yes–non-official	163	22.3	51.8
Yes–both	66	9.0	60.8
None	287	39.2	100.0
Total	732	100.0	
Portuguese Parliament			
Yes–official	5	2.2	2.2
Yes–non-official	116	50.2	52.4
Yes–both	1	.4	52.8
None	109	47.2	100.0
Total	231	100.0	
Swedish Parliament			
Yes–official	355	97.5	97.5
Yes–non-official	1	.3	97.8
Yes–both	0	0	97.8
None	8	2.2	100.0
Total	364	100.0	

requests that users should telephone the House of Commons Switchboard and ask for their MP's office, if they wish to contact their MP urgently.[17] Secondly, emails to MPs through UpMyStreet have become indirect, rather than direct communication. If a user forgets to type in his or her email address in an enquiry, the MP would not be able to reply back. Therefore, e-Democracy at the UK Parliament is mediated not only by the electronic medium but also a third party organization, namely, UpMyStreet. For users who do not know the precise email addresses of MPs and their office staff, UpMyStreet seems to be the only option for email communication with their parliamentary representative. This is in part because 'the Parliamentary web site is not able to forward any emails on to MPs or Peers' and this 'includes emails received by the House of Commons Information Office, the House of Lords Information Office and the Webmaster'.[18]

FROM RHETORIC TO REALITY: PARLIAMENTARIANS' USE OF EMAIL

Despite the fact that a fairly large number of parliamentarians in some parliaments have decided not to publish their email contact on their respective parliamentary website, most parliamentarians claim to be active users of email. The results of the questionnaire survey suggest that the vast majority of parliamentarians in Europe already use email on a regular basis. Of the 237 parliamentarians who commented on the frequency of their use of email, 93.7 per cent suggested they are 'regular' users and only three parliamentarians (1.3 per cent) declared that they do not use email at all. In the middle are 12 parliamentarians (five per cent), who said they are 'occasional users' or 'rare users'.

When asked about their use of the Internet, the majority of our parliamentarian respondents confirmed that emails are already used in a number of important areas of political communication. More specifically, as shown in Table 4, in response to the question 'To what extent do you use the Internet to communicate with other parliamentarians', 71.8 per cent (or 168) of our 234 parliamentarian respondents regarded themselves as 'regular' users. At a slightly lower rate, 61.4 per cent (or 143) of the 233 parliamentarian respondents regarded themselves as 'regular' users of the Internet in communicating with their political party/group. Meanwhile, 66.4 per cent (or 158 out of 238 respondents) considered themselves as 'regular' users of the Internet in communicating with their constituents.

TABLE 4
THE INTERNET AS A POLITICAL COMMUNICATIONS TOOL FOR
PARLIAMENTARIANS

	Number of valid respondents	Valid percentage	Cumulative percentage
To what extent do you use the Internet to communicate with other parliamentarians?			
Do not use	11	4.7	4.7
Rare use	7	3.0	7.7
Occasional use	48	20.5	28.2
Regular use	168	71.8	100.0
Total	234	100.0	
To what extent do you use the Internet to communicate with your party?			
Do not use	11	4.7	4.7
Rare use	19	8.2	12.9
Occasional use	60	25.8	38.6
Regular use	143	61.4	100.0
Total	233	100.0	
To what extent do you use the Internet to communicate with constituents?			
Do not use	9	3.8	3.8
Rare use	12	5.0	8.8
Occasional use	59	24.8	33.6
Regular use	158	66.4	100.0
Total	238	100.0	

The point that most parliamentarians use email to communicate on a regular basis is confirmed by one of our interviewees: 'We use email all the time for internal communication both within the Parliament and within the [Conservative] Party. In fact, you do not send letters to people in the Party unless there is some political reason for doing it.'[19]

Given that most parliamentarians claim themselves to be active users of electronic communication, do citizens necessarily benefit from the many advantages that email offers?

Speed of email Communication

As shown in Table 5, of the 223 parliamentarians who responded to the question of how many of the received emails are answered immediately, only a small number of them (14 or 6.3 per cent) said most (between 76–100 per cent) of the emails received were answered immediately. In comparison, nearly half (106 or 47.5 per cent) of the parliamentarian respondents could only manage to answer immediately a small proportion (between 0 and 25 per cent) of the received emails. The majority (74 per cent) of our parliamentarian respondents estimated that no more than half (between the range 0–50 per cent) of their received emails were answered immediately.

It seems that by adopting email communication some people would naturally expect an instant reply from their elected parliamentarians to their

TABLE 5
PARLIAMENTARIANS AND THEIR RECEIVED EMAILS

	Number of valid respondents	Valid percentage	Cumulative percentage
Of received emails, how many are answered immediately?			
0–25%	106	47.5	47.5
26–50%	59	26.5	74.0
51–75%	44	19.7	93.7
76–100%	14	6.3	100.0
Total	223	100.0	
Of received emails, how many are not answered?			
0–25%	136	65.4	65.4
26–50%	42	20.2	85.6
51–75%	22	10.6	96.2
76–100%	8	3.8	100.0
Total	208	100.0	
Of received emails, how many are answered personally?			
0–25%	114	50.4	50.4
26–50%	58	25.7	76.1
51–75%	32	14.2	90.3
76–100%	22	9.7	100.0
Total	226	100.0	

message. This, however, might require a change to established parliamentary practice. To many parliamentarians an email is no different to a letter. Accordingly, a reply to an email enquiry might need to go through the same process that a written reply to a letter does. Those who expect an instant reply to their email could well be disappointed by the standard practice at the UK Parliament:

> While maybe we are working on a four day cycle, getting a letter, sending, replying, we have a target of four days, sometimes we can do it in one or two days… With email, people expect instant reply, and that is not always easy to do, particularly if someone sends me an email with ten questions, which would probably take me half a day to look for the answers!… It is easy to send an email. Therefore, you tend to get some questions which possibly people would not have taken the trouble to sit down and write in a letter to you.[20]

The view of the British MP was echoed by an MEP, who suggested that the use of email has created an illusion about the speed of parliamentary communication:

> Because the Internet is a very fast medium, so everyone who is entering your webpage expects an answer in hours or minutes or something like that…but parliamentary work is also something different: you have to go to commissions, to meetings, to national assemblies, to presentations, and so on and so on, which means that you are not always in the office sitting here and answering questions that come in from the Internet. So the problem is that there is some illusion created…[21]

The gap between the expectations of email senders and the reality of snail mail replies is important and it makes us reconsider the benefits that emails are perceived to offer. In particular, if emails from young people to parliamentarians do not get an instant reply, would emails still help attract young people to communicate with their representative?

Success Rate of email Communication

To the question of how many emails never receive a reply, the answer by 65.4 per cent of the 208 respondents was up to a quarter (0–25 per cent). Another 20.2 per cent of respondents estimated that between 26 and 50 per cent of their received emails were not answered. For 10.6 per cent of the respondents, between 51 and 75 per cent of their received emails were not answered. For a small group of respondents (3.8 per cent), more than three quarters (76–100 per cent) of their received emails were not answered at all. These figures seem to confirm the concern of some e-Democracy advocates that even if we manage to get in the e-door, it is not guaranteed that we do not end up making a trip to the digital dustbin inside the Congressional office.[22] While parliamentarians might have legitimate reasons to delete messages, they do not seem to be guided by any institutional policy and parliamentary code of conduct in their handling of emails.

In the case of the UK, the parliament does have its 'Guidance for Emails', by which the parliament refuses to reply to emails if they: (a) use bad or unacceptable language; (b) are significantly indecipherable; (c) try to sell or promote a product; (d) have been sent to multiple recipients; (e) are significantly beyond the remit of the Parliament website.[23] Emails that fall within any of these categories will be deleted without having received a reply. It is worth mentioning that there is no indication whether the same guide is applicable to messages addressed to individual MPs, although UpMyStreet, the email transfer service provider, has provided a hyperlink reference to these rules. The company warns that users may not receive a reply if they do not include a full address and postcode.

Parliamentarians' Personal Attention to email Communication

In terms of who actually replies to emails, it appears that only a small proportion (9.7 per cent or 22 out of 226) of our questionnaire respondents who commented on this issue indicated that they personally answer most (between 76 and 100 per cent) of their emails. In contrast, over half (50.4 per cent) of our respondents personally answer no more than a quarter (between 0 and 25 per cent) of their emails, despite the fact that most of the questionnaire respondents agreed that emails are easy to deal with.

That only a small proportion of parliamentarians could manage to answer most of their incoming emails personally and immediately implies that the use of the Internet as a new communications tool does not necessarily help reduce the distance between politicians and citizens. It is worth noting, though, that further research is needed to distinguish between internal and external communication. In the experience of one Member of the UK Parliament, most internal emails are documents such as briefings, notes of meetings and e-circulars and these emails do not normally require a response.[24]

ETHICAL CHALLENGES OF EMAIL COMMUNICATION FOR
PARLIAMENTARIANS

In the absence of codes of conduct regarding their email communication with citizens, parliamentarians in Europe are faced with a number of ethical challenges associated with email. First, while it is versatile and convenient to use, email does not guarantee privacy of communication. Our questionnaire survey shows that 43.2 per cent of parliamentarians held the view that email is not a secure tool for communication and the lack of privacy assurance constitutes one of the most significant or significant problems of email communication (see Table 6).

Secondly, it is not always possible for the recipient to identify the email sender. A large proportion (47.4 per cent) of parliamentarians rated difficulties in ascertaining the identity of the sender as a most significant or significant problem of email communication. For parliamentarians, they need to be sure whether or not the email sender is a member of his or her constituency before a reply is considered. Many email addresses, such as those offered by Microsoft's Hotmail, Yahoo! Mail and Google's Gmail services, do not actually provide much indication about the institutional and geographical belonging of the user. During interviews we were told that parliamentarians and their office staff often needed to ask the email sender to provide full address including postcode before they consider a reply to the message. This is very much in line with the parliamentary policy in the UK regarding messages sent to the parliament's institutional email address, which requires the supply of an email sender's full contact details. By indicating their

TABLE 6

PROBLEMS FACED BY PARLIAMENTARIANS IN EMAIL COMMUNICATION WITH CITIZENS

	Number of valid respondents	Valid percentage	Cumulative percentage
Email is not a secure communication tool in terms of privacy			
Most significant problem	40	17.6	17.6
Significant problem	58	25.6	43.2
Fairly significant problem	63	27.8	70.9
Least significant problem	66	29.1	100.0
Total	227	100.0	
Not always possible to prove email sender is a constituent			
Most significant problem	35	15.4	15.4
Significant problem	73	32.0	47.4
Fairly significant problem	63	27.6	75.0
Least significant problem	57	25.0	100.0
Total	228	100.0	
Not always possible to produce signatures or attach official documents via email			
Most significant problem	34	15.1	15.1
Significant problem	68	30.2	45.3
Fairly significant problem	48	21.3	66.7
Least significant problem	75	33.3	100.0
Total	225	100.0	
You receive so many emails that it is not possible to deal with them all			
Most significant problem	123	53.7	53.7
Significant problem	35	15.3	69.0
Fairly significant problem	25	10.9	79.9
Least significant problem	46	20.1	100.0
Total	229	100.0	

postal address and postcode, the email sender could have their personal identity verified. This will also help the respective MP to find out whether the email sender was a member of his or her constituency.

Thirdly, when using email to communicate it is often difficult to produce a personal signature or attach official documents. This implies that emails have not yet rendered traditional ways of communication, such as letters, obsolete. A high proportion (45.3 per cent) of parliamentarians regarded the inability of emails to carry their personal signature or attach an official document as a most significant or significant problem.

Moreover, parliamentarians are becoming increasingly concerned with the issue of email overloading. In line with the rapid growth in the use of the Internet by the general public, parliamentarians are also faced with the growing challenge posed by the large number of emails they receive. It is not surprising that 69 per cent of the 229 respondents considered the situation in which they could not deal with all the emails addressed to them as a most significant or significant problem. Regarding the average number of emails they receive per day, as shown in Table 7, 27.3 per cent of the 238 respondents estimated that they receive 51 to 75 messages; 22.7 per cent receive 76–100 messages and another 15.5 per cent receive over 100 messages. In other words, over two thirds (65.5 per cent cumulatively) of our respondents get more than 50 email messages on average per day. Faced with the problem of email overloading one MEP said 'if I really would try to answer all my [electronic] mails I would sit here every night up to 2, 3 or 4 in the morning.'[25]

Finally, closely related to the above point, parliamentarians are falling victim to electronic spam. At an estimated total of seven billion sent worldwide each month and accounting for more than three quarters of all emails in Europe, spam refers to emails that are both unsolicited and sent in bulk to multiple email addresses and is estimated to cost the British economy alone £1.3 billion a year.[26] Among the large number of emails sent to

TABLE 7
AVERAGE NUMBER OF EMAILS RECEIVED BY
PARLIAMENTARIANS PER DAY

	Number of valid respondents	Valid percentage	Cumulative percentage
Over 100	37	15.5	15.5
76–100	54	22.7	38.2
51–75	65	27.3	65.5
26–50	44	18.5	84.0
1–25	36	15.1	99.1
0/Do not use Email	2	0.8	100.0
Total	238	100.0	

parliamentarians there are surely legitimate ones but there are also emails that are not relevant to parliamentarians' interest and work.

Table 8 shows that, among the 224 parliamentarians who rated the relevance of their received emails, some (11 or 4.9 per cent) suggested that between 76 and100 per cent of the messages sent to them were irrelevant or spam; 45 (or 20.1 per cent) of them said 51–75 per cent of their incoming messages were of this nature; 85 (or 37.9 per cent) of them thought 26–50 per cent of their messages belonged to this category. Cumulatively, nearly two thirds of respondents (62.9 per cent) said over a quarter of their emails were either spam or irrelevant to their role as an elected politician. Spam was also one of the most frequently mentioned problems during our face-to-face interviews.

Technical measures, such as software filters, would stop a high proportion of spam from getting through the parliamentary email system. Because of the high volume of spam and the increasingly more sophisticated packaging of these messages, many of them still managed to get delivered. One of the weaknesses of anti-spam software tools is their limited ability to differentiate between legitimate and illegitimate bulk emailing. For instance, in response to the recent e-petition against the proposed vehicle monitoring and road pricing policy in the UK, an email was sent out by Prime Minister Tony Blair to the 1.8 million petitioners to explain the government's position. One of the petitioners told the author that he found Tony Blair's message by accident from the 'spam' folder, rather than the inbox folder of his email account – apparently the email system automatically identified Blair's message as spam because it was sent out in bulk! This incident suggests that technical filtering of spam is less than ideal – either letting some spam messages get in or treating legitimate emails as spam.

Spam emails are generated not only from outside the parliamentary system but also from within the parliamentary system. In order to reduce the negative impact of spam, the European Parliament has circulated a Quaestors Notice admitting that regular complaints were received by the EP's technical services

TABLE 8

PROPORTION OF RECEIVED EMAILS THAT ARE IRRELEVANT OR SPAM

	Number of valid respondents	Valid percentage	Cumulative percentage
76–100%	11	4.9	4.9
51–75%	45	20.1	25.0
26–50%	85	37.9	62.9
0–25%	83	37.1	100.0
Total	224	100.0	

about internal spam.[27] Specifically, the Quaestors Notice stipulates that: (a) the electronic mail service provided by the EP is intended for work purposes and not for commercial or recreational use; (b) users at the EP are requested not to send emails in bulk that would constitute spam; (c) users are strongly advised against using the 'Reply to All' function in response to mass mailings, as this tends to launch discussion threads which the current system is unable to cope with; (d) the Quaestors reserve the right to penalise any users who fail to abide by these commonsense principles.[28] This Quaestors Notice implies that the negative impact of internally generated spam is associated with the potential loss of working hours on the one hand and threatening to overwhelm the technical capacity of the European Parliament's electronic communication system on the other hand. To be sure, nobody likes spam but many email users might have contributed to the growth of spam without realizing what they were doing.

Apart from the general ruling, the European Parliament has also compiled a list of email types that are considered equivalent to spam (see Table 9). Out of the four case study parliaments, the European Parliament appears to be the only one that has established detailed rules against internally generated spam. Unfortunately, the EP could only take action from within and it could not do very much against the wider world of spam making on the Internet.

In addition to their dislike of spam, some parliamentarians believed the use of email to communicate tends to encourage more correspondence to be generated compared to traditional ways of communication. In the words of one parliamentarian, emails could have a 'ping-pong' effect: 'whilst I will occasionally reply to an email by sending an email back,…then you get into the problem of ping-pong, because you send a reply, they send you another reply!'[29]

Because of the multiple dilemmas faced by parliamentarian email users, it is unlikely that email will replace posted letters any time soon. For some parliamentarians, 'I would much rather receive letters from constituents than emails; and we have decided in the majority of cases that if we get an email then we will print off the email and send an official written reply.'[30] If legitimate email enquiries get printed and then receive a reply by letter through the post, what is the point of sending out an email in the first place! In addition to some parliamentarians' personal preference, there is also an institutional factor, which still favours traditional modes of communication over email:

> Under this sort of system that we operate it is really a system geared up to letters, and it is easier to organise. For example at the moment all my London correspondence is being forwarded to my home address. Every-day we get a pack with the mail. And that is reasonably easy to organise. Emails are easy to lose, to be honest. You can delete them by mistake.

TABLE 9
LIST OF EMAIL TYPES CONSIDERED EQUIVALENT TO SPAM

Email type	Alternatives
Commercial/advertising/personal	
Sale or rental of goods and services	Commission's 'small ads' service; EP's information bulletin; EP's noticeboards
Goods and services wanted	Idem
Miscellaneous advertising	Idem
Car-sharing/lifts offered	
Chain letters, etc.	
Motoring-related notices	Security service
Exhibitions/lectures/invitations	
External to and not sponsored by the EP	EP's noticeboards
External but EP-sponsored	Idem
Lost and found	
Personal property	Security service; lost property service
EP trunks	Removals service
Petitions/warnings	
Internal lobbying	EP's electronic discussion forums
Computer virus warnings	Inform IT support service
Controversial subjects	
Reaction to an internal or external news item/ service/situation	EP's electronic discussion forums
Personal opinion on any subject	Idem
Reaction to an email considered equivalent to 'spam'	
Humanitarian campaigns	
Appeals for support	
NGO collections and sales	EP's noticeboards

Source: Adapted from European Parliament, 'Use of Email in the European Parliament', *The Quaestors Notice*, No. 17/03, Strasbourg, 2 July 2003.

You can see something and not recognise who it is and delete it by mistake. You do not tear up letters by mistake. You always open letters. So in most cases we would encourage people to communicate by letter.... We get an awful lot more [of] mail.... And therefore you need a system in place to deal with that. The thing is that the system that we have set up at the moment is one that deals with letters, so what happens is that an email will get printed off and put into the queue and almost certainly we will send a written reply, with a signature on the letter rather than just an email reply.[31]

To be sure, traditional post is a well-established, familiar, tried and trusted mode of communication.[32] In comparison, email communication is new, less familiar to people who are not used to reading and writing on the screen and potentially more vulnerable to human errors. In the context of the current parliamentary communication system, cautious politicians would think twice before they whole-heartedly embrace the email revolution at the expense of traditional post. Until email communication is supported by an institutional framework that is comparable with, if not more sophisticated than, the traditional set up for posted letters, email communication will remain uncertain and problematic.

CONCLUSION

The data and discussions presented in this paper show that the vast majority of parliamentarians in the British, European, Portuguese and Swedish Parliaments had a positive view about the potential of email communication for enhancing parliamentary democracy in Europe. Most parliamentarians were convinced that emails are convenient to deal with by elected politicians; they are easy to use by constituents; and emails can help attract the Internet-savvy to communicate with politicians.

Although the advantages of email communication have prompted the majority of parliamentarians at the four case study parliaments to publicise their email contact details officially, some parliamentarians have decided not to reveal their email address(es) on their respective parliament website. In the absence of any institutional policy and codes of conduct to guide their members' publicity of email contact, all the parliaments covered by this study have left the discretion in the hands of Members. Nevertheless, an overwhelming majority of parliamentarians considered themselves regular users of email – they use email frequently to communicate with other parliamentarians, with their party/political group and with their constituents.

Parliamentarians may be criticised for not making use of email at all or not making more active use of it to have a digital dialogue with citizens. Our data did show that only a very small number of parliamentarians could manage to answer just a small proportion of their emails in person. It is important to bear in mind that, in the real world, parliamentarians are faced with a plethora of challenges posed by email communication. The majority of parliamentarians believed that email systems do not offer enough protection of privacy. On the other hand, email communication often makes it difficult or impossible to ascertain the sender's identity. Meanwhile, emails, compared to letters, cannot bear parliamentarians' personal signatures, which is an important factor to making a parliamentarian's response more valued. Last but not least, email overloading has already become a major problem for parliamentarians. The burden created by email overloading is poised to offset the potential gains of email communication. Being cautiously optimistic about the future of e-Democracy, one parliamentarian remarked, 'I do not know if we are yet prepared for e-Democracy.... Not everybody is using the Internet. But the number is increasing.'[33]

NOTES
1. H. Margetts, 'E-Government in Britain–A Decade on', *Parliamentary Affairs*, 59/2 (2006), p. 262.
2. C. Di Gennaro and W. Dutton, 'The Internet and the Public: Online and Offline Political Participation in the United Kingdom', *Parliamentary Affairs*, 59/2 (2006), p. 303.
3. Interview with Maltese MEP, European Parliament, Brussels, 29 June 2005.
4. Interview with British MP, North East England, 8 August 2005.
5. Interview with British MP, North East England, 8 August 2005.
6. Interview with Austrian MEP at the European Parliament, Brussels, 28 June 2005.
7. Interview with British MP, North East England, 8 August 2005.
8. European Telework Development (ETD), 'European Parliamentarians and the Internet', April 1999, (accessed 25 May 2006) available online at: http://www.eto.org.uk/eustats/parlimnt.htm
9. S. Coleman and D. F. Norris, 'A New Agenda for e-Democracy', Forum Discussion Paper No.4, (Oxford: Oxford Internet Institute, January 2005), p. 24.
10. N. Watt, 'Blair Named on Email Shame List', *The Guardian*, 11 June 2003. The same report suggests that, while every other leader in the G8 countries was on email, Britons had to rely on posting a letter in order to contact their Prime Minister.
11. C. Leston-Bandeira, 'Impact of the Internet on Parliaments: Towards a Methodological Framework', paper presented at the Seventh Workshop of Parliamentary Scholars and Parliamentarians, Wroxton, 28–30 July 2006.
12. UK Parliament, 'Alphabetical List of Members of Parliament', http://www.parliament.uk/directories/hciolists/alms.cfm (accessed 24 May 2006).
13. Interview with British MP, North East England, 8 August 2005.
14. European Parliament, 'Replies to Questions Already Put to the Webmaster', http://www.europarl.europa.eu/tools/faq/default_en.htm (accessed 26 May 2006).
15. The third party service provider, at the time of writing, is UpMyStreet.com (www.upmystreet.com), which is part of uSwitch.com (www.uswitch.com), an online and phone based comparison and switching service company that provides price comparison on utilities, broadband and finance products in the UK.
16. UpMyStreet, http://www.upmystreet.com/commons/email/l/256.html (accessed 6 September. 2006).
17. UpMyStreet, http://www.upmystreet.com/commons/email/l/256.html (accessed 6 September. 2006).
18. The UK Parliament (2005), 'Email Guidance Notes', 10 March, http://www.parliament.uk/directories/emailguidance.cfm (accessed 6 September 2006)
19. Interview with British MP, North East England, 8 August 2005.
20. Interview with British MP, North East England, 8 August 2005.
21. Interview with Austrian MEP at the European Parliament, Brussels, 28 June 2005.
22. S. Clift, 'Share Your Views – Is the US Congress empowering the voice of independent e-citizens or throwing up the "Electronic Curtain" with e-mail changes', newswire@groups.dowire.org, 12 July 2006.
23. The UK Parliament (2005), 'Email Guidance Notes', available online at http://www.parliament.uk/directories/emailguidance.cfm
24. Personal communication with a Member of the House of Lords, UK Parliament, 30 April 2007.
25. Interview with Austrian MEP at the European Parliament, Brussels, 28 June 2005.
26. D. Brown, 'Court orders firm to pay spam victim £750', *The Times*, 6 March 2007.
27. European Parliament, 'Use of Email in the European Parliament', *The Quaestors Notice*, No.17/ 03, Strasbourg, 2 July 2003. Document obtained during interview at the European Parliament.
28. European Parliament, 'Use of Email in the European Parliament'.
29. Interview with British MP, North East England, 8 August 2005.
30. Interview with British MP, North East England, 8 August 2005.
31. Interview with British MP, North East England, 8 August 2005.
32. Note the fact that each year a significant number of letters do get lost within the Post Office system in the UK.
33. Interview with Hungarian MEP, European Parliament, Brussels, 28 June 2005.

Parliamentary Democracy Online: Lessons from Europe

XIUDIAN DAI and PHILIP NORTON

The relationship between parliament and new information and communications technologies (ICTs), in particular the Internet, is becoming ever more complicated. Among the many themes that have been addressed by the individual contributions in this volume, a number of thought-provoking points have emerged. Here, we provide a summary of the key issues.

PARLIAMENTARY AND PARLIAMENTARIANS' USE OF THE INTERNET

Our research confirms that parliaments in Europe have, to varied degrees, jumped onto the bandwagon of the Internet revolution. All of the four case-study parliaments, the British, European, Portuguese and Swedish, have adopted Internet technologies as an essential element of parliamentary communication strategy.

Our research shows that parliamentary institutions in Europe have already made, or are making, strategic responses to the opportunities offered by new ICTs. The UK Parliament, as discussed in Philip Norton's article, voted in March 2007 for each member to have an annual £10,000 'communication allowance', which may help further promote the use of new media technologies at the Parliament. The case study by Xiudian Dai on the European Parliament (EP) shows a high level of institutional commitment as demonstrated by the allocation of an annual budget of €4.36 million for ICT equipment and infrastructure at the EP, in 2006, complemented by an annual ICT maintenance budget of €470,000 from 2007 onward. We found that each of the four case-study parliaments has its own in-house ICT team responsible for the installation, maintenance and user support in relation to ICTs. Magnus Lindh and Lee Miles also noted that the Swedish Riksdag was considering raising the level of parliamentary funding so that MPs could afford to employ their own assistant.

The provision of substantial resources has enabled each case-study parliament to maintain its own computer servers, which are the central nerves of the institutional ICT environment. These parliaments have all launched email services to political and staff members, complemented by the maintenance of a parliamentary website and an intranet.

Our research found that the vast majority of parliamentarians were positive about the potentials of the Internet as a new tool for political and parliamentary communication. However, there are differences between the parliaments/ parliamentarians in their response to the digital revolution. First of all, politicians' online behaviour cannot be fully explained by 'offline' factors, as argued by Rosa Vicente–Merino in her article. While most parliamentarians at the British, European and Swedish Parliaments have their personal website hyperlinked with the parliamentary web (*via* their personal profile page), none of the Portuguese MPs had done this, at the time of our web survey.

Secondly, among those parliamentarians who have officially published their email contact(s) on the parliamentary website, there was a difference in their preference over the type of email address that they would like to use. As indicated in Dai's article on MP's use of email, 97.5 per cent of Swedish MPs have decided to publish the parliament-assigned official email address on the parliament website. This makes an interesting contrast with both the Portuguese MPs and MEPs, who were divided into roughly a half–half split in their choice of the type of email address between the official email address and private address. Fitting into none of these patterns, the UK Parliament website does not publish individual MP's full email address; instead, the majority of them (82.4 per cent) arranged to have their emails forwarded to them on a daily basis by a third-party organisation, through a hyperlink next to the MP's name.

Thirdly, it was found in our research that political parties exert a significant amount of influence over parliamentarians' use (or non-use) of the Internet. This political factor, as manifested in the cases of the British, Portuguese and Swedish Parliaments, seems to explain a lot about the reasons why parliamentarians went online (or stayed offline) and to what extent they would make use of the Internet. Due to the nature of the Portuguese electoral system that makes political parties (or Political Groups), rather than individual MPs, the most important factor, citizens tend to make more contact with party organisations than with MPs. Likewise, as argued in Cristina Leston–Bandeira's article, Portuguese MPs tend to look to their political group for disseminating information to citizens about their parliamentary work. This in part explains, from a negative point of view, why Portuguese MPs appeared to have the lowest level of Internet usage compared with politicians from other parliaments covered by our study. Through testing different models of parliamentary use of the Internet in the UK, Norton concludes that the most important factor that drives MPs to use the Internet is the desire to promote their own and their party's cause. Lindh and Miles also argue that, in the Swedish case, it is party organisations that will be the dominant factor in shaping the preferences of individual MPs over the use of ICTs.

Finally, the level of budget (or support) available to individual parliamentarians has an impact upon their decision on the use of ICTs. Although the Internet is not necessarily a difficult technology to handle by users, the process of using it, such as the maintenance of a personal website, handling of an email account, managing an online forum, etc. would require additional input in terms of staff time, funding and expertise. In some parliaments, such as the British and European Parliaments, where each parliamentarian is usually supported by several office staff and assistants, and where parliamentary provision of ICT equipment is not an issue, it is relatively easier for a parliamentarian to develop and maintain a personal website. This certainly does not apply in the case of Portugal, where it is not uncommon that one assistant supports several MPs. Although some Portuguese MPs considered the Internet as interesting, they would not have the financial means to keep an individual website. On a comparable level, in Sweden, one assistant supports five MPs.

THE IMPACT OF THE INTERNET UPON PARLIAMENT

The use of ICTs, in particular the Internet, was found in our study to have a growing level of impact upon parliamentary democracy. First of all, the Internet can have an impact upon parliament–citizen relations in the way that this medium serves as a digital bridge between a parliament and the outside world. The parliamentary website has already become an important tool for the parliament to 'market' itself to the citizens. A growing amount of information about parliamentary institutions and the legislative process is being made available on the Internet. This makes the Internet arguably more important and effective than any other type of communications technology in history, in making the parliament a transparent institution. It is not an exaggeration that the parliamentary website has already become a virtual face of the parliament.

Perhaps to a lesser degree, nevertheless no less important, the parliamentary website can also function as a communication platform between the parliament and citizens. Each of the four case-study parliaments' websites, for example, already offered facilities for citizens to contact the parliament directly either to request information or ask questions. It is worth noting, though, that online petitions did not necessarily get answered electronically; more often than not, petition questions were answered *via* the traditional post. Despite this, e-petitions serve as an additional channel for the parliament to know what citizens want to know.

Combined, the informational and communicational features of the parliamentary website have the potential to help improve the parliament's relations with citizens.

Second, inside the parliament, there are signs that the use of ICTs is showing an impact upon the institutional structure of a parliament and the established parliamentary procedures, although this is still in the early days. In Westminster, the two Houses – House of Lords and House of Commons – recently created a unified parliamentary department, for the first time in history, to deal with ICT matters. Among others, the development and use of intranet within each parliament is worth mentioning. In a highly compartmentalised institution such as the Portuguese Parliament, a single intranet is used by the whole parliament, including the Political Groups. Most of our parliamentarian interviewees had the view that the parliamentary intranet today has become indispensable to their parliamentary work. It is already the case that some types of parliamentary information and communication are available only in a digital form. A major challenge at the moment to the further digitisation of internal parliamentary communication is the requirement of parliamentarians' signature to documents. Adoption of digital signatures in the future could provide a solution to this problem. Undoubtedly, the use of intranet and email communication will lead to the reconsidering of the established parliamentary procedures.

Third, there is also evidence suggesting that the Internet can affect the relationship between individual parliamentarians and their party organisation. Leston-Bandeira found those MPs who use email to communicate with citizens can expect to develop direct contact with citizens, thus by-passing the mediation by their all-dominant Political Group. Lindh and Miles arrived at a similar conclusion that individual Swedish MPs can be electronically 'empowered' through the use of the Internet and this might lead to internal party restructuring and reduced organisational hierarchy to the advantage of the MPs, whose strong loyalties to their parties are well known. To be sure, it is becoming increasingly more difficult for parties to have an effective control over what their Parliamentary Members say through an ever-widening range of communication channels such as website, email and blogging.

It is worth noting that in the case of the UK Parliament, as Norton found, the more rebellious the MP the less likely they are to have a personal website and rebelling MPs tend to be less interested in the use of blogging compared with the party loyalists. One would expect, as hypothesised by the representative model, that rebels might be keener on pursuing the communication power offered by the Internet in order to have their voice heard.

PARLIAMENTARY POLITICS OF THE INTERNET: KEY ISSUES AND FUTURE RESEARCH

During our research a number of important issues have been raised with regard to parliamentary and parliamentarians' use of the Internet.

First, the technical features of the Internet were generally under-exploited by parliamentarians. Vicente-Merino in her analysis of parliamentarians' use of the web and Dai's study on the EP in this volume pointed out that both parliamentary and parliamentarians' websites provided very low levels of interactivity. In other words, both institutional and individual websites largely serve the purpose of information provision, rather than interactive engagement of citizens.

Second, it is rather simplistic to assume that the use of the Internet would improve efficiency and save time. On the contrary, the use of the Internet has created a widespread concern over the loss of working hours. Our research shows that, although MPs were generally positive about the potential of the Internet to become a new tool for parliamentary communication, they were also faced with the problem of email overloading. It was felt that dealing with the growing volume of electronic communication has placed additional pressure on the parliamentarians. In addition to legitimate emails from MPs' own constituency, there is also the phenomenon of spam, which accounts for a significant proportion of email flow. Most MPs found it simply impossible to deal with each message personally. In practice, as found in the cases of the British, European and Swedish Parliaments, many MPs have delegated the responsibility of email management to their office staff and assistants.

Third, there was a general lack of institutional strategies and codes of conduct for coping with the challenges posed by electronic communication. The existing institutional framework of parliamentary communication was created with reference to the old media, such as posted letters. Parliaments, such as the UK Parliament, have developed clear guidance on MPs' handling of letters from their constituents. It is unclear whether existing institutional guidance ought to be extended to email. Should emails be dealt with more speedily than letters? If yes, citizens using letters to communicate with their MP would be disadvantaged; if no, email communication as a new medium would lose its 'newness'. Some parliamentarians actually reply to email enquiries through posted letters – equity takes precedence over efficiency.

Finally, there is an ethical dimension to parliamentarians' use of ICTs. Many parliamentarians have set up their personal website using their parliamentary budget. A question to be asked here is whether these parliamentarians could use this website for advancing their personal and party political course in addition to performing their parliamentary duties. The same concern is also applicable to other aspects of ICT equipment allocated to parliamentarians such as their official email account, computers, personal digital assistant (PDA) and mobile phones. The fact that MPs in the UK may not use websites to promote their parties if the websites are maintained from public funds and MEPs, as confirmed in our interviews, were aware of the expectation that the parliamentary budget should not be used for political purposes has put politicians in a difficult position. Is it the best solution for parliamentarians to have multiple websites funded by different sources to serve different purposes?

Empirical data gathered through questionnaire surveys, web content analysis, face-to-face interviews and workshops, as presented in this volume, have demonstrated the extent to which the Internet influences parliamentary communication in its unique ways. While our findings will serve as an addition to existing knowledge and literature about the impact of the Internet upon parliamentary democracy, there is a need in future research to extend the range of case studies. In particular, the inclusion of new democracies in the European Union will make comparative studies more interesting. We also recognise the need for re-visiting the same case-study parliaments so that any change in the pattern of parliamentary and parliamentarians' use of the Internet over a period of time can be analysed.

Index

9 780415 459488